The Poverty of 'Development Economics'

DEEPAK LAL

The Institute of Economic Affairs

First published in Great Britain in 1983 by
The Institute of Economic Affairs
2 Lord North Street
Westminster
London SW1P 3LB

Second edition 1997

This third edition with a new preface published in 2002 by
The Institute of Economic Affairs
in association with Profile Books Ltd

ISBN 0 255 36519 5

Many IEA publications are translated into languages other than English or are
reprinted. Permission to translate or to reprint should be sought from the
General Director at the address above.

Typeset in Stone by MacGuru
info@macguru.org.uk

Printed and bound in Great Britain by Hobbs the Printers

CONTENTS

THE AUTHOR

Deepak Lal is James S. Coleman Professor of International Development Studies, University of California at Los Angeles, and Professor Emeritus of Political Economy, University College, London. Born in 1940, and educated at the Doon School, Dehra Dun, St Stephen's College, Delhi, and Jesus College, Oxford, he has been a member of the Indian Foreign Service (1963–66), Lecturer, Jesus College, Oxford, and Christ Church, Oxford (1966–68), Research Fellow, Nuffield College, Oxford (1968–70), Lecturer and Reader in Political Economy, University College, London (1970–84), and Professor of Political Economy, University of London (1984–93). He was a full-time consultant to the Indian Planning Commission during 1973–74, a visiting fellow at the Australian National University, 1978, and has served as a consultant to the ILO, UNCTAD, OECD, UNIDO, the World Bank, and the ministries of planning in South Korea and Sri Lanka. During 1983–84 he was an Economic Adviser to the World Bank, and then Research Administrator (1984–87), on leave from University College, London. He has been co-director of the Trade Policy Unit at the Centre for Policy Studies (1994–97), and is the Chairman of the board of advisors for the Nestlé Lecture on the developing world (1994–).

Professor Lal is the author of numerous articles and books on economic development and public policy including: *Methods of Project Analysis* (1974); *Men and Machines* (1978); *Prices for*

Planning (1980); (with P. Collier) *Labour and Poverty in Kenya* (1986); *The Hindu Equilibrium* (2 vols., 1988, 1989); (with H. Myint) *The Political Economy of Poverty, Equity and Growth* (1996), and he has edited (with M. Wolf) *Stagflation, Savings and the State – Perspectives on the Global Economy* (1986). Two collections of his essays have recently been published: *The Repressed Economy* (1993) and *Against Dirigisme* (1994). His Ohlin Memorial lectures, *Unintended Consequences: Factor Endowments, Culture and Politics*, was published in 1998. The IEA has published his *Poverty of 'Development Economics'* (Hobart Paperback 16, 1983, 2nd edition 1997), his Wincott Memorial Lecture, *The Limits of International Cooperation* (IEA Occasional Paper 83, 1990), and *The Minimum Wage* (IEA Occasional Paper 95, 1995).

PREFACE 1983

The idea for this paper arose out of concern within the Institute at the extensive and mostly uncritical attention the so-called 'Brandt Report' on International Development Issues (and its follow-up memorandum, *Common Crisis*) was attracting in Britain in contrast to the rest of the industrialised world, except perhaps for Scandinavia, the Netherlands, and Austria. It may not be a coincidence that interest in the Report has thus been highest in precisely those industrialised countries where the welfare state has reached its apotheosis. For, with its accent on wealth distribution rather than wealth creation, its vigorous advocacy of international transfers of income and collectivist regulation of the world economy, and its distrust of markets and relative neglect of incentives for private entrepreneurial effort, the Report enthusiastically embraced the assumptions and attitudes which lay behind the evolution of the most comprehensive – and increasingly unaffordable – state welfare systems of the developed world.

Be that as it may, apart from its business leaders *and* (it is gratifying to note) its professional economists, Britain seemed to like the Brandt Report. The Report was deeply concerned about poverty in the developing world and, *ipso facto*, its proposals must therefore be desirable. In 1981, 10,000 people thronged Parliament for a mass 'lobby on Brandt', with clergymen much in evidence. And Parliament appeared fascinated by Brandt. In the past three years, on a quick reckoning, the initial Report and the *Common Crisis* sequel have provoked five debates in the House of Commons, three debates in the Lords, several documents from the Commons Select Committee on Foreign Affairs, and two Government White Papers (the second promised for the end of July 1983).

The author of this paper, Deepak Lal, states at the outset that his purpose is *not* to provide a critique of the Brandt Report as such. Rather it is to expose and evaluate critically a set of beliefs – fed by a diversity of intellectual streams – about the economic development of the Third World which dominated the thinking of the Brandt Commission and which still colours the attitudes of large numbers of politicians, bureaucrats, journalists, television producers and academics in both developing and developed countries. That set of beliefs – to which Mr Lal appends the catch-all label, the *Dirigiste Dogma* – included a judgement that the tenets of standard neo-classical economic theory had little validity in the Third World and gave rise to a quest for a new 'unorthodox' economics of special application there.

The medley of theories, known collectively as 'development economics', which sprouted from this quest is the target of Mr Lal's critique. One by one, he exposes these theoretical fads for what they were – and, in some cases, still are. With devastating firepower, he trains his guns on the intricate models of 'foreign-exchange bottlenecks', 'engines of growth', 'inexorably declining terms of trade', 'dual economies', 'surplus labour', 'unequal exchange', 'basic needs' and so on – all of which, far from remaining harmless theoretical curiosities, have been translated into policy experiments, with already poverty-stricken peoples as the guinea pigs.

It is impossible in a short Preface to convey even a flavour of the richness of argument and detail of Mr Lal's study. For, in essence, it is an odyssey through the theory and practice of development over the past three decades. He has compiled a masterly, if depressing, catalogue of the serious policy errors inflicted on so many developing countries at the instigation of well-meaning interventionists who convinced themselves and others that governments not only should but could 'plan' a faster growth in living standards by supplanting market mechanisms with bureaucratic direction of resources. Looking round at the desperation of millions in Africa, Asia and Latin America, how disproportionate it seems to excuse the theorists as 'well-meaning' and leave it at that.

Two lessons emerge clearly from Mr Lal's analysis of how not to develop. First, instances of 'market failure' do not of themselves justify government intervention; there is also such a thing as 'bureaucratic failure' which makes matters worse – and bureaucratic failure is most likely to occur in poor countries with very limited supplies of trained manpower to administer controls. Secondly, the Keynesian lineage of development economics, with its macroeconomic pre-occupation with large aggregates, has diverted attention from the micro-economic role of the price mechanism in promoting an efficient use of scarce resources. If there is one piece of policy advice that can be drawn unambiguously from the development experience of the past few decades, it is: 'Get the prices right!' Nearly all the disasters have stemmed from widespread resort to 'political' pricing – most commonly in artificially maintaining exchange rates too high and prices (especially agricultural prices) too low, rationing credit at negative real interest rates, and subjecting luxury imports to prohibitively high tariffs.

Mr Lal documents at length the predictably perverse results of political prices imposed as a bureaucratic short-cut to rapid industrialisation and self-sufficiency. That they were *not* predicted at the time by the *dirigistes* who prescribed them stemmed in large part from a paternalism bordering on contempt towards the masses of the Third World. How could such wretched and ignorant folk be supposed to conform like us, either as producers or consumers, to the behavioural assumptions of orthodox neo-classical economics? But conform they do, as empirical evidence has established beyond doubt. They respond to changes in relative prices much as neo-classical economic theory foretells. As the World Bank's 1982 Development Report pointed out in its survey of Third World agriculture:

> All farmers – small, medium, and large – respond to economic incentives. Far from being 'tradition-bound peasants', farmers have shown that they share a rationality that far outweighs differences in their social and ecological conditions.

The economic development of the Third World is one of those emotion-laden subjects on which it is difficult to secure a reasoned debate. It inspires the hawking of consciences with virtually unrivalled intensity. To oppose the Brandt Report or the New International Economic Order is to be heartless and uncaring towards the poor majority of mankind, even if critics sincerely believe that the policy proposals advanced would intensify the poverty. Yet, in reality, what reasoned debate does take place is about means, not ends. All participants share the same aim of eliminating poverty and raising living standards. None has a monopoly of morality. The clergymen and other well-intentioned souls who lobbied Parliament on the Brandt Report would do well both to demonstrate more charity in their assessment of the motivation of dissenters and to make more mental effort to understand the intellectual case against the *Dirigiste Dogma*.

Deepak Lal sets out that case with clarity and rigour, and a glance at his biography will show that his considerable experience with the practical problems of development, as well as his mastery of the theory, eminently qualify him to instruct us. Although the constitution of the Institute obliges it to dissociate its Trustees, Directors, and Advisers from the author's analysis and conclusions, it offers this paper on development by a distinguished specialist confident that it will rapidly become a standard university text and hopeful that it will contribute to the improvement of policymaking in the Third World.

MARTIN WASSELL
July 1983

PREFACE 1985 (US EDITION)

This book was written in the Autumn of 1982, and first published by the Institute of Economic Affairs, London, in their Hobart Paperback series in August 1983. As it is concerned with a critical evaluation of various ideas which have influenced thinking on the problems of developing countries, a discussion of passing events is not essential for the validity of its arguments. However, the one part of the book which might seem to have been overtaken by events concerns the 'debt crisis' and the adjustments it has entailed in many middle-income developing countries. Rather than change the structure of the book, I have added a brief survey of these recent events at the end of this edition[1].

Though the UK edition of this book has been well received, there have been some misunderstandings of its nature and scope. Some readers have taken exception to the use of the term 'development economics' in the title and text. They have claimed that I use this term as a rag-bag in which are subsumed all those views concerning Third World development of which I disapprove. Moreover, as the term now describes a particular area of academic specialisation – with its own chairs, courses and students – it has been said that by castigating 'development economics' I am jeopardising the legitimate academic study of the economics of

---

1   Not included in this 2002 edition.

developing countries. Without subscribing to the protectionist nature of some of these criticisms, I would like to emphasise that it is no part of my purpose to denigrate the very important work done by many orthodox economists on the economic problems of developing countries. As I make clear in the text, the term 'development economics' is used here in Hirschman's sense and relates to a particular school of thought on the economics of developing countries, a sense I emphasise by using the term within quotation marks in the title but not throughout the text – to avoid tedium. Just as Karl Popper's *The Poverty of Historicism* was a critique of a particular type of history and not of all historical work, this book is a critique of a particular set of beliefs about Third World development and not of the whole of the economies of developing countries. In fact it is the writings in the mainstream of this branch of applied economics which I use to question the intellectual and empirical basis of one (albeit) influential school which has sought to create an unorthodox and distinct 'development economics'. In this sense there is little new or original in the book. It is more in the nature of an interpretative stock-taking of various debates on development.

However, as these debates have influenced public policy in and towards the Third World, I have above all aimed to make them accessible to the interested layman. I have consciously eschewed those detailed footnotes and fine qualifications which, whilst being the necessary hallmark of a scholarly treatise, would appear to be mere pedantry in a work such as this – which is addressed to those concerned more with getting to the heart of the matter in the various debates than with mere intellectual pyrotechnics and scholarly exegesis. For these debates deal with ideas which have public consequences. One essential function of scholarship, in my view, must be to make these ideas accessible to the general public, so that people can judge what is at stake. If as a result this book reads more like a pamphlet than a conventional work of scholarship, so be it. For as Keynes in his memoir on Alfred Marshall wrote: 'Economists must leave to Adam Smith alone the glory of the Quarto, must pluck the day, fling pamphlets into the wind, write always *sub specie temporis*, and achieve immortality by accident, if at all.'

DEEPAK LAL
Washington DC
May 1985

PREFACE 1997

This little book written in 1982 has survived the intervening years in fighting form and much to my amazement acquired quite a following. It has been translated (as far as I know) into Dutch, Portuguese and Chinese. Students have also found it useful. But it is clearly showing its age, and with the existing UK and US impressions having run out, I thought I owed readers some updating, in the form of a new edition.

But as the book has become part of the canon of its subject – both being applauded and derided (see the 1985 preface to the American edition reprinted here) – I thought it undesirable to tamper with its original form. Apart from anything else, written as it was before the almost universal victory of the market over the plan – with 1989 being as emblematic as 1789 – it retains an intensity and passion borne out of my growing impatience with the *Dirigiste Dogma* and the damage it had done to the economic prospects of the vast bulk of humanity contained in the Third World. This partly accounted for its success, and as the *dirigiste* beast has at best been quelled rather than slain, it may still be useful – particularly for students and general readers interested in the Third World – to be aware of the arguments deployed by *dirigistes* in the past and the counters to them.

So, rather than rewrite it completely, or add addendums to each chapter, I have instead added a new self-contained Postscript, which besides a brief statistical updating, deals with the ideas and events which have impinged on development policy since the early 1980s, and briefly discusses some emerging themes in both thought and action concerning economic development.

This is based in part on a paper written at the request of the Commission on the Future of the Bretton Woods Institutions in 1994. The extensions and revisions were done whilst I was a fellow of the International Center for Economic Research at Turin in May 1996. My gratitude to both institutions.

Finally, given the bouquets and brickbats hurled at the book, any author, whilst gratefully clutching the bouquets, is sorely tempted to hurl back the brickbats. Though it would have been easy to deal with my critics in the manner of Operation Desert Storm, I have resisted the temptation. In any case, in a book aimed at the general reader, such scholastic battles would be pedantic. As with the original edition, my aim in the Postscript is to provide the interested layman with an accessible account of the issues and debates on development which have emerged since the book was first written.

DEEPAK LAL

Los Angeles and Turin

June 1997

PREFACE 2002

It is five years since the revised and expanded edition of this book appeared. Since then, the Asian, Russian and Brazilian crises may seem to have undermined its arguments. In particular the Asian crisis, which took the stripes off many of the region's tigers, may seem to provide a cautionary tale of the perils of the outward-looking development path advocated in this book, where years of progress can seemingly be wiped out by some young traders on Wall Street pushing a few buttons on their computers. It may be useful to see why this inference is unwarranted by briefly outlining the causes of this crisis. These were threefold.

The first cause was the quasi-fixed exchange-rate regimes in many of the countries. It is increasingly becoming clear that in a world with a globalised capital market only two exchange regimes are viable: a fully floating exchange rate or one rigidly fixed as in the currency boards of Hong Kong and Argentina. The reason is that these are the only ones which allow automatic adjustment to external and internal shocks without any need for any discretionary action by the authorities.[1] This lesson has now been learned by many countries in the Third World.

---

1   See Lal (1993), Ch. 6. It should also be noted that there is currently a movement in Latin America to replace domestic currencies by the dollar. It is argued that even with a currency board (as in Argentina), domestic interest rates are above US levels, which unnecessarily raises the cost of borrowing – particularly by the

The second cause was a systemic flaw in the 'Asian' model of development. A central feature of this model – as seen most clearly in Korea, but presaged by the development of Japan – is a close linkage between the domestic banking system, industrial enterprises (particularly the biggest) and the government.[2] The fatal danger of this 'model' is that, by making the banking system the creature of the government's will, tremendous moral hazard is created in the domestic banking system. The banks have no incentive to assess the creditworthiness of their borrowers or the quality of the investments their loans are financing, since they know that no matter how risky and over-extended their lending, they will always be bailed out by the government. This can lead in time to a mountain of bad paper and the *de facto* insolvency of a major part of the banking system, as has happened in both Korea and Japan – not to mention the corruption that is inevitably involved in this type of development.

But, as the example of the US savings and loans crisis shows, this mess in the banking system can ultimately be cleared up, as is happening in the region, with both Korea and Thailand bouncing back, although the continuing political turmoil in Indonesia leaves its prospects a cause for continuing concern.

Its problems are due in part to the role of the International

---

government. Dollarisation would lower interest rates to US levels and also allow domestic firms and the government to issue long-term international bonds. But, as is argued on pp. 219–23 below, concerning the misalignment of real exchange rates, these potential cost savings of dollarisation have to be set against the adjustment costs that are avoided in a flexible exchange-rate system in the face of negative shocks which require a real exchange-rate adjustment. The higher interest-rate costs associated with this regime can be looked upon as an insurance premium which avoids these costs on the downside.

2   See pp. 236–9 below.

Monetary Fund (IMF): the third of the causes of the Asian and other crises. The problem of moral hazard for the domestic banking system created by the 'Asian' model has been aggravated by the actions of the IMF and the entrance of foreign bankers as lenders into the newly liberalised capital markets. Of the three types of capital flows that can be distinguished – direct foreign investment, portfolio investment and bank lending – the income and foreign-currency risk of the first two types is shared by both the lender and the borrower, as the 'investments' are denominated in domestic currency. By contrast, foreign bank loans are usually denominated in dollars and the interest rate is linked to the London interbank offered rate (LIBOR). This means that, if faced by a shock requiring a devaluation, the domestic currency burden of the foreign bank debt rises *pari passu* with the changing exchange rate. If the debt is incurred by the private sector, this rising debt burden need pose no problem for the country, for if the relevant foreign banks run, the borrowers can always default on their debt.

But now, enter the IMF. Ever since the 1980s debt crisis, foreign banks faced by a default on their Third World debt have argued that this poses a systemic risk to the world's financial system, and have asked in effect for an international bail-out to prevent this catastrophe. The IMF has been more than willing to oblige. For, since the Bretton Woods adjustable peg exchange rate regime – which the IMF was set up to manage – ended, with President Nixon's closing of the gold window in the early 1970s, the IMF has been like a character in Pirandello's play, *Six Characters in Search of an Author*. The debt crisis of the 1980s provided one play for it to perform in, the rocky transition of the Second World from plan to market another, and the Mexican, Asian and Brazilian crises a third. The IMF has increasingly become the international debt collector for foreign money-centre banks, as well as an important tool of US foreign policy.[3] It should be shut down.[4]

As regards the 'Asian model', it is dead. Countries are increasingly recognising that what is derisively called the Anglo-Saxon model of capitalism is the only viable one in the long run. It alone can deliver that prosperity that a globalised economy offers in an unprecedented manner to all its participants. Hence, most of the countries involved in the crisis are adopting its institutional bases: transparent financial systems and deeper financial markets which allow hedging of foreign-currency risk, and either a floating or rigidly fixed exchange-rate regime as in a currency board or a monetary union. Those bucking the trend will increasingly learn the costs in terms of the future prosperity of their citizens.

DEEPAK LAL
Los Angeles and London
May 2002

---

3   Soon after the Indonesian acceptance of the IMF's programme, Jakarta was plastered with pictures of a grinning managing director of the Fund standing over a little brown man signing away his country. An understandable nationalist backlash could easily turn into the economic nationalism that in the past has blighted Asia's economic prospects.

4   As should its Bretton Woods twin, the World Bank, as both have passed their sell-by dates. See D. Lal: *Unfinished Business*, Oxford University Press, New Delhi, 1999, ch. 9.

ACKNOWLEDGEMENTS

The research on which this book is based formed part of a project, funded by the Nuffield Foundation, on the New International Economic Order. My collaborator on this project was Professor David Henderson of University College, London. I would like to thank Martin Wassell and Michael Solly of the Institute of Economic Affairs for editorial help well beyond the call of duty.

The postscript bringing the story of changing ideas and events up to mid-1996 is based on a paper entitled *From Plan to Market – Post War Evolution of Thought on Economic Transformation and Developments*, written at the request of the Commission on the Future of the Bretton Woods Institutions. Further research was done whilst I was a fellow of the International Centre for Economic Research in Turin.

D.L.

SUMMARY

- From the end of World War II to the early 1970s, most Third World countries adopted 'inward-looking' policies. These policies then began to break down until 'collapse of the Second World' in the late 1980s started a '… breathtaking worldwide movement from the plan to the market'.
- The new liberal international economic order is similar to that in the nineteenth century in that free movement of goods and capital prevails. But immigration controls inhibit the movement of labour.
- In the last twenty years, the performance of developing countries as a whole relative to OECD countries has much improved, largely because of big improvements in East Asia and South Asia. The 1980s were a 'lost decade' for sub-Saharan Africa and Latin America, though prospects are now better in both areas.
- Liberalising Third World countries can now attract private portfolio and direct investment. Except for Africa, private flows of foreign capital are more important than official 'aid'.
- The final 'nail in the coffin' of the 'old' development economics was realisation of the immense corruption it breeds. *Dirigisme* necessarily results in politicisation and rent-seeking.
- The 'consensual policy package' of the 1990s stresses state

provision of essential 'public goods'; otherwise, economic activity should be left to private agents.

- Past *dirigisme* led to disorder, eroding the state's fiscal base. The resulting crises were often the occasions for liberalisation. A 'big bang' approach to liberalisation may be necessary: otherwise the state may cease liberalising once the immediate crisis is past.

- 'Adjustment with a human face' is the new slogan of those who want to create Western-style welfare states in the Second and Third Worlds at a time when First World countries, where the welfare system has been captured by the middle classes, are embarking on reform.

- Many East Asian countries have shown that mass poverty can be eradicated within a generation. 'A market-based liberal economic order can cure the age-long problem of structural mass poverty.'

- Western democracy embodies tensions between the notions of the state as a civil association and as an enterprise association. The '… mere transfer of Western forms of governance and their attendant ideology is as unlikely to secure the market in the Third World as it is in the First.'

TABLES AND FIGURES

The Poverty of 'Development Economics'

INTRODUCTION

A study of the history of opinion is a necessary preliminary
to the emancipation of the mind.

J. M. Keynes: *The End of Laissez-Faire*, p. 16

This paper aims to outline and critically assess the validity of a set
of beliefs about the economic development of the Third World
which still colours the thinking of a large number of politicians,
bureaucrats, journalists and academics in both developing and developed countries. A diversity of intellectual streams has fed these
beliefs. Though it is neither possible (given the space) nor feasible
(given my competence) to trace the lineage of this body of opinion
with thoroughness, I hope to provide an account of some of the
different elements which have helped form what I will call the *Dirigiste Dogma*. Its most recent and influential statement is contained in the Brandt Commission's report, *North-South: A
Programme for Survival*.[1] My purpose, however, is not to provide
another critique of the Brandt Report[2] but to expose and evaluate
the view of the world (and more particularly the ways to change it
under government aegis) which underlie Brandt and much other
thinking about the problems of developing countries. Nor shall I

---

1   Brandt Report 1980 [32], and Brandt Commission 1983 [33].
2   P. D. Henderson [75].

seek to explain in terms of psychology and history the continuing popularity of the *Dirigiste Dogma* amongst those concerned with promoting the economic development of the Third World. I have done this elsewhere.[3]

I shall instead argue the intellectual case against this body of thought. If practical men think such an enterprise is of mere academic interest, they should recall Keynes's famous dictum about the influence of ideas on policy.[4] Further, as I hope to show, the appeal of the *Dirigiste Dogma* rests in part on the belief that it has a sound analytical and empirical basis. It may astonish the layman to learn that it is the technical justification of the *Dirigiste Dogma* which is most open to question. Though the ensuing technical critique is a prerequisite to understanding the precise objections to this body of thought, neither the level of abstraction nor the economic concepts are inherently difficult.

Though some proponents of the *Dirigiste Dogma* convey the impression of being the exponents of a 'new economics', they are, rather, prisoners of a particular interpretation of orthodox theory for which their derogatory term is 'neo-classical'. It is not in my view useful to force the participants in these debates on development – as some have sought to do – into the Procrustean bed of ideological categories such as 'Right'- or 'Left-wing'. Though the resulting flow of adrenalin might add to the drama of imaginary battles across the ideological barricades, it is unlikely to illumine

---

3 Lal [108].

4 'Practical men, who believe themselves to be quite exempt from any intellectual influences, are usually the slave of some defunct economist. Madmen in authority, who hear voices in the air, are distilling their frenzy from some academic scribbler of a few years back ... soon or late, it is ideas, not vested interests, which are dangerous for good or ill.' (J. M. Keynes, *The General Theory of Employment, Interest and Money*, Macmillan, 1936, pp. 383–4.)

the logic of the alternative views on development, and in particular the role of government to promote it, which is my primary concern. For as a recent writer on the history of economic ideas has noted:

> The disadvantage of most attempts at an ideological classification of economic theories ... is that they tend to reveal more about the political and intellectual bias of the compiler and his mentors than about the methodological qualities of the economic doctrines thus labelled.[5]

One final caveat is required in setting the stage for our debates on development. Since my chief concern is to delineate the various ideas which have fed the *Dirigiste Dogma*, I shall have to identify the views of particular economists which provide its intellectual ballast. This does not, however, imply that all those who have supplied ammunition for the *dirigiste* armoury would accept the purposes for which it has been deployed. Nor will I be able to outline the various qualifications. these economists rightly made in putting forward ideas which subsequently seemed to gain a momentum of their own. What I am hoping to do is to offer a general outline of the ideas which form the essential intellectual baggage of the *Dirigiste Dogma*, and to argue that many of them – in the light of both the logical criticisms they have attracted and the experience of developing countries during the last three decades – are not soundly based.

The first Chapter sets out the major elements of the *Dirigiste Dogma* and traces the broad outlines of the ideas which underlie it. It argues that, despite the explicit rejection of orthodox economics, its policy-oriented branch – namely, welfare economics –

---

5   Phyllis Deane [50], p. 216.

provides the intellectual critique of *laissez-faire* and a *prima facie* justification for *dirigisme*. Modern developments In welfare economics, however, also supply the necessary antidote to *dirigisme*. For this reason, more space than may seem warranted is devoted to certain abstract arguments which the general reader may find tiresome. But part of my case is that the economists who have fed the *Dirigiste Dogma* have neither stuck to their last nor provided an alternative framework for the design and assessment of public policies. It is therefore important to set down the logic of modern welfare economics, since this gives the necessary framework for assessing the analytical claims of *dirigiste* panaceas in four important debates on development.

The first of these concerns the role of foreign trade and official or private capital flows in promoting economic development. The second concerns the role and the appropriate form of industrialisation in developing countries, and the third the relationship between the reduction of inequality, the alleviation of poverty and so-called different 'strategies' of development. A central feature is the massive increase in labour supply flowing from the rapid growth of population in most developing countries in recent years, which is alleged to pose a chronic though undefined 'unemployment' problem. Fourthly, underlying all these is the more fundamental debate about the role of the price mechanism in promoting development. Those who reject orthodox economics have usually also emphasised the importance of central planning to supplant rather than supplement the workings of the market mechanism.

1 THE DIRIGISTE DOGMA

The essential elements of the *Dirigiste Dogma*, as I see them, can be briefly stated. The major one is the belief that the price mechanism, or the working of a market economy, needs to be supplanted (and not merely supplemented) by various forms of direct government control, both national and international, to promote economic development. A complementary element is the belief that the traditional concern of orthodox micro-economics with the allocation of given (though changing) resources is at best of minor importance in the design of public policies. The essential task of governments is seen as charting and implementing a 'strategy' for rapid and equitable growth which attaches prime importance to macro-economic accounting aggregates such as savings, the balance of payments, and the relative balance between broadly defined 'sectors' such as 'industry' and 'agriculture'.

The third element is the belief that the classical 19th-century liberal case for free trade is invalid for developing countries, and thus government restriction of international trade and payments is necessary for development. Finally, it is believed that, to alleviate poverty and improve domestic income distribution, massive and continuing government intervention is required to redistribute assets and to manipulate the returns to different types of labour and capital through pervasive price and (if possible) wage controls – and through controls which influence the composition of commodities produced and imported – so that scarce resources are used to meet the so-called 'basic needs' of the poor rather than the luxurious 'wants' of the rich.[1]

In arguing against the *Dirigiste Dogma*, I do not want to question the objectives it ostensibly seeks to serve, namely, equitable and rapid growth to make an appreciable dent, as quickly as possible, in poverty in the Third World. My case is that the means proposed are of dubious merit. Nor, more importantly, am I arguing for *laissez-faire*. That doctrine, as Keynes noted in his famous book, *The End of Laissez-Faire* – better known, alas, for its title than its contents – has been under attack by orthodox economics since John Stuart Mill.[2]

Sadly, many *dirigistes* implicitly contrast their set of beliefs as an alternative to one based on *laissez-faire*. The real issue between them and orthodox economists, however, is the form and extent of government intervention, not its complete absence. Just as Keynes noted that it was not the economists but 'the popularisers and vul-

---

1   Nurkse [167, 168], Myrdal [162], Hirschman [78], Balogh [14], Rosenstein-Rodan [177], Chenery [39], Prebisch [171], Singer [192], and Streeten [202] are notable amongst many others who would consider themselves to be non-neo-classicals and whose writings have been influential in providing various elements of the *Dirigiste Dogma*. There has, however, always been some opposition to these views: Haberler [65, 66]. Viner [210], Bauer and Yamey [18], Schultz [181].

2   Keynes [91], p. 26. Nor is 'the phrase *laissez-faire* to be found in the works of Adam Smith, of Ricardo or of Malthus. Even the idea is not present in a dogmatic form in any of these authors'. (p. 20) 'This is what the economists are *supposed* to have said. No such idea is to be found in the writings of the greatest authorities.' (p. 17) 'Some of the most important work of Alfred Marshall – to take one instance – was directed to the elucidation of the leading cases in which private interest and social interest are not harmonious. Nevertheless, the guarded and undogmatic attitude of the best economists has not prevailed against the general opinion that an individualistic *laissez-faire* is both what they ought to teach and what in fact they do teach.' (p. 27)

garisers'[3] who spread the *laissez-faire* doctrine, so it cannot be assumed that many distinguished contemporary economists whose views have fed the modern-day *Dirigiste Dogma* thereby necessarily subscribe to it themselves. It has been argued that Marx was not a Marxist, nor Keynes a Keynesian, and many a thinker who has nourished the *dirigiste* stream is not a *dirigiste*. This paper, therefore, is concerned with correctly interpreting not so much what particular economists meant as what they have been taken to mean by a wider lay public. For it is the latter which ultimately determines the climate of opinion in which alternative policies are judged and implemented.

The alleged irrelevance of orthodox economics

Before we enter the more important debates on some of the specific beliefs of the *dirigistes*, it remains to chart the major intellectual foundations of the broad claim that *dirigisme* is required to promote development. Fortunately, an important contributor to this set of beliefs has recently characterised the major underlying assumptions which distinguish what he labels 'development economics' from both orthodox economics and various Marxist and neo-Marxist schools of thought on the economics of developing countries. Albert Hirschman distinguishes the various schools in terms of what he calls the 'mono-economics' claim and the 'mutual-benefit' claim.[4] According to Hirschman, the mono-economics claim asserts that traditional economics is applicable to developing countries in the same way as it is to developed ones; the mutual-benefit claim asserts that 'economic

---

3   *Ibid.*, p. 17.

4   A. Hirschman [79].

relations between these two groups of countries could be shaped in such a way as to yield gains for both'.[5] Whilst orthodox economics accepts both claims and neo-Marxists are presumed to reject both, Hirschman argues that development economics rejects the mono-economics but accepts the mutual-benefit claim – unlike Marx himself who would have accepted the mono-economics but rejected the mutual-benefit claim!

It is chiefly the influence of Hirschman's 'development economics' that I wish to counter in this paper – though, to the extent there are many neo-Marxist influences on policies for and towards the Third World, I shall be dealing briefly with these too. Despite Hirschman's categorisation, development economics is closer to the neo-Marxists than to orthodox economics in its view of the mutual-benefit claim. For development economics, mutual gains can be realised only after legitimate departures from the orthodox case for free trade which must be enforced by government action both nationally and internationally. In practice, therefore, whilst not going as far as the neo-Marxists in their desire to smash the whole world capitalist system based on 'unequal exchange',[6] development economists nevertheless accept that developing countries are 'unequal partners'[7] in the current world trading and payments system, and that the rules of the game of the liberal international economic order must be changed to serve their interests.

---

5   *Ibid.*

6   The title of an influential neo-Marxist work by A. Emmanuel [55].

7   The title of a well-known collection of papers by Lord Balogh [14].

The Keynesian heritage

The analytical and empirical bases of development economics were provided by the Keynesian 'revolution' in economic thought and the experience of the developing countries during the Great Depression of the 1930s. While the next Chapter will consider the lessons that were drawn from the latter, a few remarks are required here about the Keynesian lineage of development economics and the revolt against orthodox economics that it was supposed to represent.

The specific Keynesian remedy for curing mass unemployment during a depression was soon seen to be irrelevant to developing countries which, unlike developed ones, did not face unemployment of both men and machines. Rather, their problem was too few 'machines' adequately to employ the existing 'men'.[8] All the same, in contrast with the orthodox economics castigated by Keynes, Keynesian modes of thought were seen as relevant to the problems of development. Both the central theoretical concern of Keynesian economics – namely, the determinants of the level of economic activity rather than the relative prices of commodities and factors of production – and its distinctive method – namely, national income-expenditure analysis – were enthusiastically adopted by development economics. The allocation of given resources, a major concern of orthodox economics, was considered of minor importance compared with the problems of increasing material resources – subsumed in the portmanteau term 'capital' – and of ensuring their fullest utilisation.

These Keynesian modes of thought also led to an implicit or explicit rejection of the primary role assigned by orthodox eco-

8   V. K. R. V. Rao [173].

nomics to changes in relative prices in mediating imbalances in the supply and demand for different 'commodities' – including not merely such obvious commodities as carrots and clothes, but also hypothetical composite 'commodities' such as 'savings', 'investment' and 'foreign exchange'. Changes in income were substituted as the major adjustment mechanism for bringing supply and demand into balance. This neglect of the role of the price mechanism was usually justified by assumptions based on casual empiricism: that there were limited possibilities for consumers in developing countries to substitute different commodities as their relative prices changed since their consumption consisted of bare essentials, for which no substitutes existed; and that producers could not substitute cheaper inputs for more expensive ones because, by assumption, their production techniques required inputs to be used in fixed proportions. The implicit or explicit assumption of what economists call 'limited substitutability' in both consumption and production meant the downgrading of a large part of the role played by relative price changes in adjusting the demand and supply of different commodities and factors of production to each other.

Moreover, the concentration on macro-economics, flowing from Keynesian modes of thought, required thinking in terms of aggregates of different 'commodities'. At its simplest, this conceptual aggregation necessitates an assumption that the relative prices of real-world commodities which constitute the aggregate composite 'commodity' remain unchanged during the period of analysis. As a result, the neglect of the price mechanism, except for the relative 'prices' of these composite 'commodities', is almost inbuilt into macro-economic thinking. Though undoubtedly useful for certain analytical and policy purposes, there is a consequent temptation – not often resisted in development economics – to ignore micro-economic problems altogether in the design of public policies.

The concentration on macro-economics was further aided by the spread of national income accounting and the establishment of statistical offices in most developing countries to provide the necessary data. Though the resulting information has considerably improved our quantitative knowledge of developing countries, it has also given a fillip to a particular type of applied economics research in both developed and developing countries which can be termed 'mathematical planning'. Building on the work of Tinbergen and his associates[9] in estimating statistical macro-economic relationships (from the 'time series' data supplied by the national income statisticians), and on the work of Leontief in refining 'input-output analysis' to describe the inter-relationships in the production structure of an economy, development planning seemingly acquired a hard scientific and quantifiable character.

The Leontief input-output system,[10] building as it did on the Soviet practice of 'material balance planning', ignored relative price changes by assuming that the inputs for producing particular real-world commodities were required, for technological reasons, in fixed proportions. The typical development plan first laid down a desired rate of growth of aggregate consumption. Then the quantities of different commodities required in fixed proportions, either as inputs into production or outputs for consumption, were derived from an input-output table for the economy. Since such

9   J. Tinbergen [208].
10   W. Leontief [124], H. Chenery *et al.* [41].

plans were presented in terms of desired quantities of production of various goods, their implementation most often entailed direct controls on production, including state provision of some goods considered either too important to be supplied by the private sector or unlikely to be produced by the private sector in the planned amounts.

The neglect of welfare economics

The final intellectual strand in the making of development economics was a neglect of the one branch of economic theory which provides the logic to assess the desirability of alternative economic policies, namely, welfare economics. This was due partly to its rejection of much of micro-economics, and partly to what was seen as the inherently limited applicability of conventional welfare economics, whether of the classical sort as systematised by Pigou or the 'new welfare economics' of Hicks and Kaldor. Broadly two types of objections were raised against this branch of economics, and they continue to be echoed in contemporary development economics. The first concerned its ethical foundations, the second the real-world relevance of its assumptions about consumers' tastes and producers' technology.

It is important to assess these objections, and the current status and scope of welfare economics, for three reasons. First, because welfare economics provides 'the grammar of arguments about policy':[11] those seeking to argue the case for increased government intervention might have been expected to use it to bolster their claims. Secondly, the development of what is labelled

---

11   F. H. Hahn [67].

'second-best' welfare economics (below, pp. 52–5) was stimulated in part by the problems and debates about developing countries.[12] Thirdly, and equally important, the analytical framework for assessing the claims of the *Dirigiste Dogma* (as of *laissez-faire*) is provided in large part by welfare economics, and it is therefore necessary to outline briefly the logic of this important branch of economics.

Welfare economics is concerned with two general classes of practical questions: *(a)* the measurement of real national income,[13] and *(b)* the efficiency and equity of particular economic outcomes, including the scope for improving them through various instruments of public policy. These are the very issues of assessing economic performance and designing policies to improve it which lie at the heart of the practical debates on development taken up in later chapters of this paper. I turn, therefore, to outlining the development of modern welfare economics, albeit very cursorily, to show how it lends *prima facie* support to the *Dirigiste Dogma*, but also to show why this support is deceptive.

One major strand of objections to welfare economics concerns its ethical foundations. For our purpose, it is sufficient to note that such objections are related to questions about the distribution of income – whether and how the distributional effects of economic change should be accounted for in measuring changes in aggregate economic welfare.[14] Not surprisingly, there is no consensus to date on these normative issues since the ethics of income distribution

12 J. M. D. Little and J. A. Mirrlees [142, 143], P. Dasgupta–S. Marglin–A. Sen [49], A. H. Harberger [70], Little, Scitovsky, Scott [145].

13 Sen [190] provides a lucid survey of the issues.

14 A. K. Sen [189].

and other political aspects of the good society remain controversial. But does that invalidate the positive welfarist conclusions about the so-called optimum conditions for production and exchange required for an efficient allocation of resources? There are some development economists who believe so.[15] This is to misunderstand the logic of modern welfare economics, however, and to derive illegitimate inferences from the legitimate criticism that it might be ethically blinkered. For, as we shall see, the most useful results of modern applied welfare economics do not depend upon accepting a particular ethical viewpoint. They are 'the logical conclusions of a set of consistent value axioms which are laid down for the welfare economist, by some priest, parliament or dictator',[16] whilst, as far as the *Dirigiste Dogma* is concerned, the policies it has engendered have aided neither efficiency nor equity nor liberty in the Third World.

The theoretical attack on *laissez-faire*

It remains to chart the second set of objections to welfare economics which have also led to its neglect in development economics. These concern its 'positive' aspects. The basic theorems of welfare economics – rigorously derived in the 1950s by Professors Arrow and Debreu – show that, in a perfectly-competitive economy with universal markets for all commodities distinguishable not only by their spatial and temporal characteristics but also by the various conceivable future 'states of nature' under which they could be traded (that is, there is a 'complete' set of fu-

---

15 P. Streeten and S. Lall [206], for instance.
16 Little [135], p. 80.

tures markets for so-called 'contingent' commodities[17]), a *laissez-faire* equilibrium will be Pareto-efficient in the sense that, with given resources and available technology, no individual can be made better-off without someone else being made worse-off. Since, however, this competitive, Pareto-efficient equilibrium may not yield the distribution of income considered socially desirable according to the prevailing ethics, government intervention may be necessary to legislate the optimum income distribution even in a perfectly competitive economy with complete markets. If government can levy lump-sum taxes and disburse lump-sum subsidies, the perfectly competitive economy can attain a full 'welfare optimum'.

It is, however, premature to cheer this rigorous establishment of the case for a *laissez-faire* economy in which the government's role (apart from providing a legal framework to enforce property rights and maintain law and order) is confined to lump-sum redistributive measures (assuming the unmodified distribution conflicts with prevailing ethical norms). For, as many critics of the price mechanism have been only too ready to point out, the conditions (or assumptions) for establishing it are extremely unrealistic. Broadly, the assumptions fall into those required for (a) perfect competition and (b) universal markets.

Perfect competition depends on stringent assumptions about the tastes of consumers and the nature of producers' technology. First, there must be no interdependencies in either consumption or production not mediated through markets (that is, there must

---

17 A 'contingent commodity', for instance, would be 'ball-bearings' for delivery on 16 September 1995, where the future price is conditional upon whether or not industrial production in Indonesia is 20 per cent above average that month.

THE POVERTY OF 'DEVELOPMENT ECONOMICS'

be no so-called 'external effects', such as keeping up with the Joneses or emitting smoke which damages the output of a nearby laundry). And, secondly, there must not be too many industries with decreasing costs of production (that is, 'increasing returns' in production must not be large relative to the size of the economy) since these are likely to lead to monopoly. Development economists have emphasised the importance of 'externalities' and 'increasing returns' in developing countries.[18] Though usually asserted rather than empirically demonstrated, it has led them to reject the argument for a market economy implicit in the notion of a perfectly-competitive Utopia.

These two assumptions are not nearly as unrealistic,[19] however, as the other major one required to show the Pareto-efficiency of a *laissez-faire* competitive economy, namely, the existence of universal markets. The lack of markets for all current and future 'contingent' commodities is likely to be the fundamental cause of so-called 'market failure'. Externalities pose problems essentially because of the difficulty (if not impossibility) of creating a market for them even though, conceptually, they can be readily identified as 'commodities' (factory smoke, for example, is a commodity, but also a 'bad' for which there is no market). The reason is that, to create a market in any commodity, non-buyers must be excluded from obtaining it. Exclusion may be technically impossible or prohibitively expensive, in terms of resource costs. for most 'externalities'. Where exclusion is possible, there may be so few buyers and

---

18   Rosenstein-Rodan [177], T. Scitovsky [184], Hirschman [78], Chenery [39].
19   Many externalities can he dealt with by suitable taxes and subsidies; and, in an open economy, the potential danger of decreasing-cost industries becoming monopolistic is reduced by foreign competition.

sellers in the market for the externality that it cannot be perfectly competitive.[20]

The difficulty of establishing markets in these commodities reflects what are broadly termed the costs of making transactions attached to any market or indeed any mode of resource allocation. Transaction costs include the costs of exclusion as well as those of acquiring and transmitting information by and to market participants. They drive a wedge, in effect, between the buyer's and the seller's price. The market for a particular good will cease to exist if the wedge is so large as to push the lowest price at which anyone is willing to sell above the highest price anyone is willing to pay.

Apart from making it difficult to deal through an unfettered market with externalities, these transactions costs will also limit the development of futures markets for all commodities. Thus, far from being an apologia for the *laissez-faire* doctrine, as many suppose, modern welfare economics provides the precise reasons why, even in the absence of distributional considerations, a real-world *laissez-faire* economy is not likely to be Pareto-efficient – because (a) it is unlikely to be perfectly competitive, and (b) it will certainly lack universal markets.

---

20 Arrow [7] cites the example of the lighthouse keeper who knows exactly 'when each ship will need its services, and ... abstract from indivisibility (since the light is either on or not). Assume further that only one ship will be within range of the lighthouse at any moment. Then exclusion is perfectly possible; the keeper need only shut off the light when a non-paying ship is coming into range. But there would be only one buyer and one seller and no competitive forces to drive the two into a competitive equilibrium. If in addition the costs of bargaining are high it may be most efficient to offer the service free'. (p. 15)

The limits of rational *dirigisme*

Thus, even if income distribution is disregarded, there would seem to be a *prima facie* case for government intervention. It would be absurd, however, to jump to the conclusion that, because *laissez-faire* may be inefficient and inequitable, any form of government intervention thereby entails a welfare improvement. For transactions costs are also incurred in acquiring, processing and transmitting the relevant information to design public policies, as well as in enforcing compliance. There may consequently be as many instances of 'bureaucratic failure' as of 'market failure', making it impossible to attain a Pareto-efficient outcome.

Let us consider the question of legislating for the optimal income distribution in an otherwise competitive, Pareto-efficient economy. If government could levy *lump-sum* taxes which were inescapable and could not be avoided by economic agents altering their otherwise efficient choices, it could achieve the full welfare optimum. If, for example, income differences were related to the inescapable abilities of individuals, and there was an unambiguous and readily available (at low cost) index of these abilities, a lump-sum tax/subsidy system based on differential abilities would allow the full welfare optimum to be achieved (in a perfectly-competitive economy with complete markets). Clearly, such a system is not feasible because of the costs of acquiring the necessary information.

By contrast, a tax/subsidy system based on *income* differences which aimed at legislating for a desired income distribution would not be lump-sum because it would affect the choices individuals make at the margin between work and leisure. By distorting the initial, *ex hypothesi,* efficient allocation, the income-based tax/subsidy system, though improving the distribution of income, would impair the productive efficiency of the economy. The feasible instrument of government intervention would mean that the welfare gain from an improved distribution could only be obtained by inflicting a welfare loss in the form of lower productive efficiency. Because of the 'bureaucratic failure' inherent in the inability of government to introduce a lump-sum tax-subsidy system, a full welfare optimum is not attainable even with government intervention. All that can be achieved is a 'second-best' optimum where the *net* gain from the distributional gain and efficiency loss are at a maximum.

The same argument applies to government intervention to correct market failures in any real-world economy which is not perfectly competitive or which lacks complete futures markets. There are few, if any, instruments of government policy which are non-distortionary, in the sense of not inducing economic agents to behave less efficiently in some respects. Neither markets nor bureaucrats as they exist can therefore be expected to lead an economy to a full welfare optimum. The best that can be expected is a second-best.

Given that the optimum is unattainable, the relevant policy problem becomes that of assessing to what extent particular government interventions may raise welfare in an inherently and inescapably imperfect economy. The Utopian theoretical construct of perfect competition then becomes relevant as a reference point by which to judge the health of an economy, as well as the remedies suggested for its amelioration. Since improvements will not necessarily entail a movement towards the perfectly-competitive theoretical norm, evaluating the likely consequences of alternative policies in an imperfect economy becomes a subtle exercise in what is nowadays termed 'second-best welfare economics'.

An early theoretical contribution by Lipsey and Lancaster correctly argued that, in an imperfect economy, the restoration of some of the conditions which would exist under perfect competition would not necessarily result in an improvement in welfare.[21] This insight was unfortunately taken to mean that there was no way in which the effects on economic welfare of alternative piecemeal policies to improve the working of the price mechanism or to alter the distribution of income could be judged. Many took it to imply that, since every economy is imperfect, welfare economics (and by implication microeconomics) was irrelevant in the design of public policy. One of the major analytical advances of the last two decades, prompted by the problems of developing countries, has been to show that this is not so.[22] Specific examples of the application of modern second-best welfare economics are given in the next chapters, and the Appendix (p. 181) provides an outline of the logic of the exercise.

The major point to note is that no general rule of second-best welfare economics permits the deduction that, in a necessarily imperfect market economy, particular *dirigiste* policies will increase welfare. They may not; and they may even be worse than *laissez-faire*. Moreover, any economic justification for a *dirigiste* policy not based on the logic of second-best welfare economics must be incoherent, and akin to the miracle cures peddled by quacks which are adopted because of faith rather than reason. The burden of the case against the *Dirigiste Dogma* in its application to developing countries is that, though in many instances some forms of *dirigisme* might have been beneficial had they been feasi-

---

21 Lipsey and Lancaster [133].
22 Two sets of applications of this theory are in Little and Mirrlees [142], and W. M. Corden [46].

ble, the *dirigiste* policies actually adopted (either because they were considered the only feasible ones, or else because the relative costs and benefits of alternative policies were never examined) have often led to outcomes which, by the canons of second-best welfare economics, may have been even worse than *laissez-faire*. The conclusion, therefore, of this theoretical tour is that the very analysis which seemingly establishes a *prima facie* intellectual justification for the *Dirigiste Dogma* provides, in its fullness, the antidote!

2 THE EXTERNAL ENVIRONMENT I: TRADE

Introduction

The Great Depression and World War II cast a long shadow over the prospects of developing countries in two important ways. First, and probably more importantly, it was the period when new protective devices – quantitative restrictions on imports and exchange controls to manage the balance of payments – were first employed on a wide scale in both developed and developing countries. This gave legitimacy in many developing countries to a form of protection which, arguably, was more harmful to their long-run development than the tariff commonly employed in the 19th century. Secondly, the collapse of world trade, and in particular of commodity prices, in the inter-war period engendered a deep pessimism about the export prospects of the Third World in the post-war years.

Although development economics, with its emphasis on increasing returns, might have been expected to highlight the importance of international trade and investment in the development process, on the lines of the arguments developed by Adam Smith, it became, instead, the leading purveyor of an autarkic model of development. Theory and practice seemed mutually to reinforce each other, and many developing countries turned inwards during the 1950s and early 1960s in an attempt to foster a hothouse, import-substituting industrialisation behind protective walls which were higher, more uneven (and hence arbitrary) in terms of the protection they afforded different commodities, and more comprehensive, than anything imagined by the mercantilists castigated by Adam Smith.

During the 1960s, both the empirical and analytical basis of what had become the conventional wisdom in development economics was challenged. A few countries – South Korea, Taiwan, Hong Kong and Singapore – had flouted the conventional wisdom much earlier, and others – Thailand, Malaysia, Brazil, and Mexico, for instance – soon followed suit. The resulting differences in performance between those countries which adopted so-called 'outward-looking' as opposed to 'inward-looking' development policies have since become one of the best-documented and -analysed aspects of the economics of developing countries, and have contributed to the fall of development economics lamented by Hirschman. But ideas – good or bad – never die in economics; with the 'slumpflation' of the 1970s and early 1980s, the old ideas of 'trade pessimism' are being resurrected in new guises. The purpose of this Chapter and the next is to review these challenges to the standard economic case for an open trading and payments system.

The first protectionist wave

Ragnar Nurkse was the leading light of the post-war challengers to the liberal trading and payments order. He maintained[1] that the historical role international trade had played in the 19th century as an 'engine of growth' for the new countries of white settlement –

---

1   Nurkse [168].

the USA, Canada, Argentina, and Australia – was no longer available to the Third World. Basing his case entirely on demand factors (echoing the dominant Keynesianism of the time), he argued that this was because the demand for tropical products in developed countries could not be expected to grow sufficiently to enable Third World primary producers to raise their national incomes through this source at a satisfactory rate. Unlike some others, he did not object to the Third World seizing the trading opportunities available, but he was pessimistic about their future availability. In contrast to grain (which, according to Nurkse, was the basis of the white-settler colonies' prosperity), the demand for tropical products in developed countries did not, so he maintained, rise in line with the growth in their incomes because the 'income elasticity' of demand for these goods[2] was low. There was also the danger that synthetic substitutes would be developed for many tropical products. Neither did he expect Third World countries to be able to export manufactures, partly because of the difficulties of producing them efficiently in developing countries, and partly because of the protectionism he thought such exports would provoke in developed countries. He therefore advocated what he called 'balanced growth', Which was in effect a policy of forced import substitution to meet home demand for imports.

Nurkse's reading of history and his predictions about the future both proved false. The view that international trade was an engine of growth in the 19th century for the countries of new settlement has been questioned by Irving Kravis.[3] His essential argument is that economic growth depends primarily upon internal

---

2   The income elasticity measures the percentage change in the quantity of the good that is demanded as a result of a percentage change in income.

3   Kravis [94].

factors. International trade provides an extension of the domestic opportunities available for converting domestic resources into goods and services required for either investment or consumption. Furthermore, by widening the market for a country's products, it enables it to produce on an efficient scale goods which have decreasing costs of production. Finally, and probably most important of all, exposure to international competition is the best anti-monopoly policy in practice, and prevents the development of high-cost industries.

Most of these benefits concern the efficient use of available resources and hence the supply side of the economy. The demand factors with which Nurkse and others were so preoccupied cannot be of such importance because the development experience of countries which shared in the 19th-century expansion of trade was so different. For instance, Australia seemed to develop whereas Argentina did not, despite similar resource bases, 'white' populations (Argentina had none of the problems of assimilation posed for other countries in Latin America by a 'backward' indigenous population), and a similar stimulus from the rise in export demand for their major primary products. Thus, as Kravis emphasises, though a strong external demand for a country's exports may be helpful, it

is neither a necessary nor sufficient condition for growth or even trade to play a helpful role in growth ... The term 'engine of growth' is not generally descriptive and involves expectations which cannot be fulfilled by trade alone; the term 'handmaiden of growth' better conveys the role that trade can play.[4]

Moreover, even if Nurkse was right in claiming that the

---

4   *Ibid.*, p. 869.

Table 1 **Some historical statistics of trade and growth in the world economy**

(A) 1850–1913	% per annum
Per capita world output	1.5–2.0
Volume of world trade	3.5–4.0

(B) 1913–1948	
Per capita world output	2.0
Population	1.0
Productivity	1.0
Volume of world trade	0.5

(C) 1948–1973	
Per capita world output	5.0
Population	2.0
Productivity	3.0
Volume of world trade	7.0

(D) Composition of world trade, 1913–73 (Percentage shares)

	1913	1953	1973
All commodities	100	100	100
Agricultural products	45	36	21
Mineral products (including fuels)	8	13	14
Manufactures	44	49	63
of which			
Machinery & transport equipment	7	18	33
Textiles & clothing	14	6	6

(E) Shares of world merchandise exports, 1955–79

Country group	1955	1965	1970	1980(a)
All developing countries	27.3	20.2	18.4	21.4
Low-income	5.6	3.4	2.5	1.9
China	1.4	1.0	0.7	0.9
India	1.4	0.9	0.6	0.4
Other	2.8	1.5	1.1	0.6
Middle-income	21.7	16.8	19.5	19.5
Major exporters of manufactures	6.8	5.7	6.2	8.0
Other oil importers	6.9	4.1	4.3	3.9
Oil exporters	8.0	7.0	5.4	·7.6
High-income oil exporters	2.1	2.5	2.4	10.2
Industrial non-market economies	8.5	10.9	10.1	7.9

Country group	1955	1965	1970	1980(a)
Industrial market economies	62.1	66.5	69.0	60.5
Europe	36.1	41.1	42.5	38.5
Japan	2.1	4.5	6.2	6.5
United States	16.5	14.6	13.6	10.9
World	100.0	100.0	100.0	100.0
Memorandum item				
World exports (billions of dollars)				
Current prices	94	186	313	1,995
1978 prices	420	542	821	1,405

(a) Includes some estimates.
Sources: (A) from Lewis [130], pp. 32–3.
(B–D) Blackhurst *et al.* [31], pp. 5, 7–8, 64.
(E) World Bank, *World Development Report 1982* [214], p. 26.

external demand for exports from developing countries in the 19th century was their major engine of growth, his expectation that such a process would fail to function in the post-war world was wildly off the mark, as Table 1 shows. World trade, and in particular the volume of exports from developing countries (excluding fossil fuels), grew at historically unprecedented rates. Nurkse's pessimism about the slowing down of the trade engine was engendering inward-looking policies in the Third World just when the engine was beating faster for developing countries than even the wildest expectations based on 19th-century experience.

The terms-of-trade myth

This pessimism about the export prospects of developing countries was coupled with the thesis propounded by Prebisch and Singer[5] that both theory and historical fact demonstrated an

---

5   Prebisch [171], Singer [192].

Table 2a **GNP per capita and its annual growth rate, by region, 1950–75**

| | | ——— GNP per capita ——— | | |
| | Population, 1975, million | — 1974 US $ — 1950 | 1975 | Annual growth rate 1950–75, % |
Region	(1)	(2)	(3)	(4)
South Asia	830	85	132	1.7
Africa	384	170	308	2.4
Latin America	304	495	944	2.6
East Asia	312	130	341	3.9
China, People's Republic of	820	113	320	4.2
Middle East	81	460	1,660	5.2
Developing countries	2,732	160	375	3.4
Developing countries excluding China	1,912	187	400	3.0
Developed countries[a]	654	2,378	5,238	3.2

a All OECD countries except Greece, Portugal, Spain and Turkey.
Sources: Columns 1 and 3: data tapes of *World Bank Atlas* (1977). Column 2: estimated by applying growth rate of GDP per capita, 1950–60 (World Bank, *World Tables 1976*), to figures for 1960 GNP per capita (*Atlas* tapes). Column 4: Computed from columns 2 and 3.

inexorable tendency for the commodity terms of trade of developing countries (particularly primary producing ones) to decline. Though both the theoretical and factual bases of these views have subsequently been questioned,[6] it has not prevented UNCTAD and numerous development experts – as well as spokesmen for developing countries – from continuing to assert them with vigour. The terms-of-trade myth provided *dirigistes* with further arguments for turning their backs on the orthodox case for freedom of international trade and payments. If, as was asserted, the existing trade system led to a pattern of specialisation in which the gains from productivity increases in Third World primary production

---

6   R. E. Lipsey [134], Spraos [195].

Table 2b **Annual growth rate of GDP per capita, selected countries, 1870–1975, %**

Country	1870–1913 (1)	1913–50 (2)	1950–75[a] (3)
Argentina	1.5	0.7	1.9
Brazil	n.a.	2.4[b]	3.7
Chile	n.a.	0.6	0.7
China (Taiwan)	n.a.	0.7	5.3
Colombia	n.a.	1.4	2.0
Egypt, Arab Republic of	n.a.	0.2	1.4
Ghana	n.a.	1.2	0.7
Greece	n.a.	−0.1	5.4
India	0.7	0.2	1.5
Malaysia	n.a.	2.2	2.6
Mexico	1.2[c]	1.2[d]	2.7
Pakistan	0.7	0.2	n.a.
Peru	n.a.	1.5	2.5
Philippines	n.a.	0.1	2.8
Spain	n.a.	−0.3	5.1
Yugoslavia	n.a.	0.9[e]	4.7
Unweighted average	1.0	0.8	2.8[f]

a Growth of GNP per capita
b 1920–50.
c 1877–1910.
n.a. Not available
d 1910–50.
e 1909/12–50.
f Weighted average = 2.0.

Source: David Morawetz [157].

were transferred to advanced countries whereas productivity gains in the latter's manufacturing activities accrued to their own inhabitants, the Third World must shun it as likely to result in their immiseration. Import-substituting industrialisation was again the panacea offered.

The most extreme form in which these ideas coalesced was the assertion by Myrdal and Balogh[7] that, contrary to the classical

---

7   Myrdal [162], Balogh [14].

view that a liberal international trade and payments régime yielded mutual benefits to all the partners, it was really a 'zero-sum game' enabling the rich advanced countries to prosper at the *expense of* the poor backward ones. Invoking the Biblical dictum:

> For unto every one that hath shall be given, and he shall
> have abundance: but from him that hath not shall be taken
> away even that which he hath,

Myrdal[8] suggested that the liberal international system would inevitably make the rich richer and the poor poorer.

The economic history of the past three decades has not borne out his confident prediction. This is so whether we compare the performance of developed *versus* developing countries or of different developing countries – which, far from being a homogeneous group, differed considerably in living standards in 1950. Table 2 should convince the unconvinced. The richest region in the developing world in 1950 (Latin America) grew more slowly, in terms of per capita income, than the second poorest region (East Asia – excluding Communist China), which also grew faster than the richest region in the world (the developed world). Furthermore, among *individual* developing countries for the period 1950–75, 'there seems to be no clear relation between initial income level and subsequent growth rates'.[9]

Pessimism about the trade prospects of developing countries was soon formalised into so-called 'two-gap' models of development by McKinnon and by Chenery and Strout.[10] These seemingly provided a rationale to continue the trade and exchange controls

---

8   Myrdal, *op. cit.*, p. 46.

9   Morawetz [157], p. 17.

10 R. McKinnon [149], Chenery and Strout [42].

which had been universally adopted in developing countries by the 1950s. Of equal importance was the rationale they provided for massive inflows of foreign capital, in the form of foreign aid, as the panacea for development.

The foreign-exchange bottleneck

In these two-gap theories, Nurkseian pessimism was carried to its logical extreme by assuming that the export proceeds of developing countries could not be increased.[11] Furthermore, it was assumed that domestic production required imported inputs, in the form of capital and intermediate goods, in set proportions. Production could not, therefore, be increased above that determined by the quantity of imports which the fixed export earnings could finance. Even if a country was willing to save and invest a larger proportion of its income to finance growth, it would not be able to transform the savings into higher income and output because of the inexorable limit set by the 'fixed' export earnings. The incremental savings could not be transformed into the foreign exchange to finance the import requirements of additional investment. The country was now stuck in a foreign-exchange bottleneck.

This chronic balance-of-payments constraint on a country's development could not be cured by the orthodox means of raising the price of foreign exchange (through a devaluation) to induce an increase in the supply of and a reduction in the demand for this 'good' which was inhibiting growth. For both these effects had been ruled out by assumption. Either the volume of

---

11   For a critique of these foreign-exchange bottleneck-type models, Lal [101].

exports was limited by world demand; or an increased volume of exports could be sold only at declining prices on world markets without any rise in foreign-exchange earnings. Thus, raising the price of foreign exchange would not increase its supply, whilst the technologically-fixed import requirements of domestic output meant that, for any quantity of output, raising the price of foreign exchange would have no effect on demand for it. The only available options were for government to husband its fixed foreign-exchange fund for use in 'essential' industries and to seek to augment it through concessional foreign loans and grants.

In practice, the response of developing countries to this presumed chronic shortage of foreign exchange divided into two broad categories. Some sought to disprove the major assumption that export earnings must remain constant by diversifying into export lines where neither stagnant world demand nor declining world prices posed a problem. Given the vast expansion in world trade, particularly in manufactures (Table 1), these developing countries (primarily in East Asia) found that the pessimism about their export prospects – particularly in the simpler and more labour-intensive manufactures – was completely unwarranted. Moreover, the resulting specialisation to harness their comparative advantage yielded income growth (particularly for unskilled labour – their most abundant resource) unimaginable by even the most fervent classical proponents of the gains from trade.

The second category of countries accepted the pessimism about trade prospects and set about breaking the foreign-exchange bottleneck by reducing the import content of domestic production and consumption through direct control of imports and inducements for import substitution, regardless of the real resource costs to their economics. India was a prime example. Instead of breaking the foreign-exchange bottleneck, such protectionist developing countries found that their trade and exchange-rate policies made foreign exchange even scarcer. This was for two reasons. First, as a result of paring imports to the bone, the import requirements of their economies became insensitive to the price of foreign exchange. Since the only imports allowed were of goods which, though essential for domestic production, could not conceivably be produced within the country, demand for them became insensitive to changes in their price. This, however, was the effect of policy, not technology.

At the same time, the trade controls they had set up to husband a presumed fixed quantity of foreign exchange introduced a bias against exporting and thus retarded the growth of potential exports – of the sort, for instance, being so successfully developed by the East Asian countries. This was because the heavy, often prohibitive, protection made it unprofitable to produce for anything but the domestic market.

Protection is the equivalent of a subsidy to the output of import-competing industries financed by a tax on users. The relative profitability of export industries declined with protection, and producers were naturally more reluctant to expand output as compared with producers of import substitutes. Furthermore, since protection raised the price of importable goods generally, users switched some of their expenditure to the now relatively cheaper exportable goods. The pressures for a lower supply and higher domestic consumption of exportable goods together reduced the overall incentive to export. The resulting failure of export earnings to rise to finance the growing import demands prompted a further tightening of the screw of import controls, with a further bias against exports. This continued until imports had been limited to

THE POVERTY OF 'DEVELOPMENT ECONOMICS'

their bare minimum and the policies introduced to ensure it had prevented any growth in exports. The foreign-exchange shortage, which might initially have been cured by the normal means of a devaluation, was then chronic. Through the policies it engendered, the foreign-exchange gap had become a self-fulfilling prophecy by *leading* to the very retardation of export earnings and the irreducibility of minimum import requirements which were its premises.[12]

The orthodox counter-attack

Balance-of-payments fears lay at the root of most protective policies in developing countries, for which the foreign-exchange 'gap' theory usually provided an *ex post* rationalisation. Development economics has, however, also been a vocal advocate of protection on *dirigiste* grounds, supposedly flowing from the inefficiencies of *laissez-faire* discussed in the last Chapter; for the cases for free trade and *laissez-faire* have come to be closely identified.[13] In particular, it was argued that the ubiquitous presence of external effects in production and consumption, and of increasing returns in production, invalidated the case not merely for laissez-faire but also for free trade.[14] Though there were a few powerful and cogent voices dissenting from this popular view in the 1950s and early 1960s, it was not until the mid-1960s that, building on the work of Meade, Haberler and Viner,[15] Harry Johnson and two Indian econ-

---

12 For evidence from a large number of countries in support of the assertion, Little, Scitovsky and Scott [145], Bhagwati [24], Balassa [11, 13], Krueger [98].

13 Myrdal [162], pp. 152–3, for example.

14 Nurkse [167], Scitovsky [184], Hirschman [78], Myrdal [162], Balogh [14].

15 Meade [148], Haberler [64], Viner [210].

omists, Jagdish Bhagwati and V. K. Ramaswami,[16] pubfished sem-inal work rigorously establishing why the case against *laissez-faire* did *not* destroy the case for free trade. Their contribution was, in fact, a standard application of the theory of the second best. They showed that most arguments for protection based on the need to correct distortions in the working of the domestic price mecha-nism (discussed in Chapter 1) were arguments for *domestic* taxes-cum-subsidies and *not for protection* which, far from curing the perceived ills, could make matters worse.

Theory is quite rightly never sufficient to persuade the scepti-cal. The final attack on the protectionist aspects of the *Dirigiste Dogma* was made by detailed empirical and historical studies of the effects of different trade and industrialisation policies followed by a number of countries failing broadly into the two groups iden-tified above. These studies were pioneered by Ian Little, Tibor Scit-ovsky and Maurice Scott at the OECD in the mid-1960s and extended by Bela Balassa at the World Bank, by Juergen Donges's group at Kiel University, and by Jagdish Bhagwati and Anne Krueger for the US National Bureau of Economic Research (NBER).[17] They have provided an impressive empirical validation of the theoretical case against protection and for the view that, even though *laissez-faire* may not be justifiable, free trade remains the best policy for developing (and developed) countries.

This demonstration follows from the canons of second-best welfare economics outlined in Chapter 1. Let us suppose, as is

---

16 Bhagwati and Ramaswami [26], H. G. Johnson [86].
17 Little, Scitovsky, Scott [145], Balassa [11], Bhagwati [24], and Krueger [98]. These include detailed studies of India, Turkey, the Philippines, South Korea, Chile, Colombia, Egypt, Ghana, Pakistan, Taiwan, Israel, Brazil, Mexico, Argentina, and Singapore.

often asserted, that the real cost of labour to industry in developing countries overstates its true social cost, either because industrial wages are set at an uneconomically high rate by trade union pressure or, more subtly, because industrial labour is drawn from family-owned farms worked with family labour. Since the new industrial labourer is likely to have been receiving the *average* product of labour on the family farm, which includes a share in the implicit rent accruing to the family-owned plot of land, his previous earnings, and therefore the industrial wage he will demand, will be higher than his *marginal* contribution to agricultural output. Since all industry presumably suffers from this disability of having to pay wages higher than the opportunity cost of labour, it is argued that, without government intervention but with free trade, industrialists who would be perfectly able to compete against imports if they had to pay only the true social cost of labour will be undercut by foreign competition. Protection will offset this disadvantage. Clearly, however, because the root of the trouble lies in a 'distortion' in the market for labour, the way to maximise welfare would be to provide a wage subsidy to industry which eliminated the distortion at its source. (Though, for the reasons set out in Chapter 1, if the subsidy cannot be financed through lump-sum taxes, the *costs* of the distortionary taxation required to finance the subsidy must be set against the *benefits* from the removal of the primary distortion to gauge the *net* change in economic welfare.)

If such a wage subsidy is not feasible for administrative reasons, it may be 'next-best' to offer a production subsidy to manufacturing industry as a whole. This will be worse than a wage subsidy since it does not attack the primary problem of too high an industrial wage. It will lead to a choice of production techniques which are more capital-intensive than is socially desirable. But it would be better than protection offered, say, through a general uniform tariff because of the further by-product distortions caused by the latter, the most important of which is the bias against exports. In terms of the *net* effect on economic welfare, the tariff will be worse than various other domestic tax-subsidy instruments to deal with the primary distortion. It may turn out that the net effect is a *loss*. If it is then argued that, for whatever reason, the superior tax-subsidy instruments cannot be used, it may be best to *do nothing*.[18]

The effective rate of protection

The above argument has been couched in terms of the effects of a uniform tariff. Yet the actual form of protection used in most developing countries has been the quota. The widespread use of quantitative restrictions to ration imports has had many more harmful side-effects, compared with tariffs. The *nominal* rate of protection, which measures the percentage increase in the prices of imports in the home market caused by the protective device, varies according to the size of the quota allocation to a particular good, domestic demand for it, and whether or not there is a legal or black market for either the import licence itself or the imports it authorises. Unlike the tariff, therefore, quotas effectively cut the link between domestic costs and prices and those in international markets. More seriously, whilst the nominal protection becomes uncertain and changeable from year to year, the *effective* rates of protection offered to producers of different commodities become

---

18   For a lucid account of this modern theory of trade and welfare, Corden [46].

highly differentiated and variable, their relative values bearing no relationship to any known principles of rational government intervention.

Effective rates of protection differ from nominal rates wherever there are internationally-traded inputs in the production of an import-substituting commodity and the tariff rates on the output and the tradeable inputs differ. Thus if cloth is produced with imported cotton and domestic labour, each of which accounts for half the value of cloth at international prices, a *nominal* tariff of 50 per cent on cloth and a zero rate on cotton implies an *effective* protection of 100 per cent of the domestic value-added by labour. If, however, the imported input and the competing imports bear the same tariff, the nominal and effective rates will be the same. In practice, most developing countries (and developed ones, too) cascade their tariff structures, with inputs usually attracting lower tariffs than final output. This produces much higher effective protection than may be apparent from a perusal of nominal tariff rates. Since it is the *effective* rates of protection which determine the relative profitability of producing different goods, the pattern of resource allocation thereby induced has often been based on no economic rationale, and has frequently conflicted with the stated aims of government.

Let us consider the example of India. After the first serious foreign-exchange crisis in 1956–57, a complex system of quota restrictions on imports was instituted. All requests to import were subjected to administrative scrutiny, and even the most petty imported items required a licence. Moreover, import licences were not available for goods which could be produced within India. This led to effective rates of protection which exceeded 200 per cent on average, with a high variability of rates around the average. Imports of capital and intermediate goods were allowed whilst those of consumer goods were banned, with the consequence that, on balance, effective rates of protection of, and hence incentives to invest in, the indigenous consumer goods industries were higher – an outcome at odds with the stated policy of promoting heavy industry! And since the effective rates of exchange were much higher for importers than exporters, there was a bias against exports.

The practice of screening requests for imports according to the so-called 'indigenous availability' criterion[19] led to the complete insulation of domestic production from foreign competitive pressures which, coupled with an overall excess of demand in the economy, meant that producers had little incentive to reduce costs. The rules of thumb used by administrators to allocate imports were based on the principle of 'fair' and 'historic' shares and the installed capacity of producers. The result was a freezing of the relative outputs and market shares of industries and firms. It also led to excess capacity as producers rushed to expand ahead of their requirements, knowing that their licensed capacity determined their import allocation and hence volume of production. Most heinous of all, because the structure of effective protection implied a relative cheapening of capital goods, producers had an incentive to choose relatively more capital-intensive methods of production at the expense of employing more labour. At the same time, the protection afforded to industry as a whole artificially raised the price of manufactured inputs into the agricultural sector relative to the price of its output. This had deleterious effects on agricultural growth.

---

19 This criterion stipulated that any good which could be supplied by a domestic producer could not be imported.

One distortion requires another

At various stages during the 1960s and early 1970s these harmful effects of the existing trade control system – particularly on exports – had begun to be acknowledged, even in India. Export incentives, aimed at redressing the bias against exports, were introduced. Not surprisingly, the partial removal of this bias led to a spurt in exports, as economists who were not mesmerised by foreign-exchange bottlenecks had always predicted.[20] In many instances, however, the *dirigiste* impulse was not stifled. India matched its highly complex and bureaucratic system of import allocation with an equally complex system of export incentives. The major instrument used was an import entitlement for exporters in the form of import licences whose premium provided the exporter with a subsidy, The effect was to create a host of new distortions in the export sector.[21] A simple policy of export maximisation was pursued; any producer wishing to export found a government willing to grant him an import entitlement whose premium was sufficient to equalise the relatively high domestic costs and low foreign prices of his product. Since the entitlements were usually tied to the import content of exports, these schemes subsidised import-intensive exports rather than those with a high domestic value-added. The widespread practice of over-invoicing exports, coupled with different effective exchange rates for exports and imports, meant that a number of goods with a high import content were exported for a lower foreign currency return than the foreign currency cost of the imports embodied in them! India thus ended up by pursuing import substitution and export promotion with-

---

20   Bhagwati and Srinivasan [27].
21   Lal [116].

out reference to economic costs, guided only by the belief that 'India should produce whatever it can and India should export whatever it produces'.[22] The inefficiency, waste, and corruption that the Indian trade control system has engendered are incalculable. But, at least for *this* Indian, it stands as a lasting and appalling monument to the ideas of Nurkse, Prebisch, Singer, Myrdal, Balogh, *et al.*

The incontrovertible case for trade liberalisation

To summarise, the Nurkseian scepticism about the desirability of free trade for the Third World was based on three explicit or implicit assumptions. The first was a pessimistic assumption about the external obstacles to Third World growth which gave rise to the myth of the foreign-exchange bottleneck. Secondly, economic agents in developing countries were assumed to be congenitally shortsighted[23] in basing their investment and production decisions on current, static advantage rather than on emerging, dynamic, comparative advantage. Finally, it was assumed that bureaucrats and planners could both predict the dynamic comparative advantage of a country more efficiently than private agents and ensure through detailed state intervention that production and investment patterns conformed to it. The experience of a host of developing countries analysed in the OECD, World Bank, and NBER studies referred to above (p. 69) shows the error

22 Bhagwati and Desai [25], p. 466.
23 Thus Balogh [14] states: '*In the poor areas* the difficulties and imperfections of effective decision making, the lack of entrepreneurial ability and capital, vitiate the assumption that potential fields of investment opened up by trade will automatically be exploited.' (p. 16)

of all three assumptions. *The obstacles to the growth of developing countries' exports are largely internal, not external; economic agents in these countries have reacted to the distorting incentives created by protectionist régimes of trade control much in the way that standard economic theory predicts; planners have often shown a lack of foresight which would have swiftly bankrupted a private agent!*

The case for liberalising financial and trade control systems and moving back to a nearly free trade régime is now incontrovertible. Most countries, however, including the East Asian success stories – apart from Hong Kong – retain *dirigiste* spots in their trade policies, and few have seriously attempted the full-scale liberalisation that is required.[24] The essential elements of a liberalisation programme can be briefly stated. As a first step, existing import quotas must be replaced by equivalent tariffs, followed by a phased programme of tariff reductions over a number of years to minimise the unavoidable costs of adjustment to producers and workers in inefficient industries. To smooth the transition to more efficient economics also demands a proper sequence of reform of domestic banking systems and of monetary management. These issues are not discussed here since they are still highly controversial and would also take us too far afield. But their vital importance in reversing the harmful internal policies of developing countries should be borne in mind.[25]

The political difficulties on the path to more efficient domestic policies should not be minimised. They stem largely from the manifold vested interests in the maintenance of the trade control system which it has itself created by providing large windfall

---

24　Little [137, 138].

25　R. McKinnon [150], McKinnon and Mathieson [151].

profits to those lucky, influential or corrupt enough to obtain various licences,[26] and by fostering an inefficient structure of industry where the current incomes of so many producers contain an element of rent derived from the existing system of controls. A courageous, ruthless and perhaps undemocratic government is required to ride roughshod over these newly-created special interest groups. It is not surprising, therefore, that most countries (as the NBER studies document) have attempted liberalisation in a half-hearted way only to backslide as the political and economic difficulties of the bumpy transition are encountered.[27]

The new wave of protectionism

As if the transition to more liberal trading policies was not difficult enough, new siren voices in the current slumpflationary condition of the world economy are suggesting that it may be both unnecessary and undesirable. The slowing down of world trade and growing protectionism in the West are being exploited to establish a new version of the Nurkse-Prebisch-Singer thesis about the inimical effects of 'Southern' dependence on 'Northern' economies. The earlier misconceptions that trade serves as the engine of growth in development and that the terms of trade (this time the so-called 'factoral' rather than the 'commodity' terms of trade) are inherently biased against the South are both being revived.

The most surprising recruit to this band is Sir Arthur Lewis, whose earlier historical work[28] was of profound importance in

---

26 Krueger [97] has aptly labelled this phenomenon as the creation of a rent-seeking society.

27 Krueger [98].

28 Lewis [128, 130].

dispelling the notion advanced by Nurkse, Prebisch and Singer that Third World primary producers (as opposed to the grain producers of the area of white new settlement) did not benefit from the 19th-century liberal trading order. In his 1980 Nobel lecture, Lewis presented the most sophisticated version of a new 'trade pessimism'.[29] As with Nurkse, the centrepiece of his analysis is a demand-oriented theory of development where trade serves as an engine of growth. He bases this theory on the following empirical regularity:

> The growth rate of world trade in primary products over the period 1873 to 1913 was 0.87 times the growth rate of industrial production in the developed countries; and just about the same relationship, about 0.87, also ruled in the two decades to 1973. World trade in primary products is a wider concept than exports from developing countries, *but the two are sufficiently closely related for it to serve as a proxy*. We need no elaborate statistical proof that trade depends on prosperity in the industrial countries.[30]

Reidl[31] has recently tested Lewis's thesis that developing countries' exports are driven by external demand, as well as the postulated empirical relationship between the two. The words in italics from Lewis's Nobel lecture contain by no means an innocuous assumption, for one of the profound changes in the structure of developing countries' exports has been that, whereas manufactures accounted for only 10 per cent of their non-fuel exports in 1955, that share had risen to over 40 per cent by 1978 (Table 3). Primary product exports can no longer serve as a proxy for developing

---

29   Lewis [131].
30   *Ibid.*, p. 556.
31   Reidl [175].

country exports, as Lewis asserts. Nor, except for sub-Saharan Africa, is the picture much altered by descending from these aggregate heights. For, though there are major differences in the export structure of different developing countries, with manufactures now accounting for 75 per cent of the exports of the four East Asian super-performers, most of the countries in South Asia, plus Egypt, Brazil, Mexico, Tunisia and some smaller Latin American countries – accounting for about two-thirds of the population of the developing world – have also raised the share of manufactures in their exports (on a trade-weighted basis) from an average of 15 per cent in 1950 to above 50 per cent in 1978.

Nor does Lewis's link coefficient of 0.87 between the rate of growth of Northern 'industrial production' and Southern exports fare any better once both the time period (1953–73) and Southern exports are disaggregated. Broadly speaking, the hypothesised link is unstable over time, and the only primary commodities for which it seems to obtain are tea and sugar. For manufactures, the dominant and growing element in Southern exports, Reidl concludes that 'the evidence ... suggests that supply rather than demand factors have principally determined LDC export performance in manufactures'.[32] This is also the conclusion of the numerous historical studies of the trade and industrialisation policies of Third World countries cited earlier (p. 69).[33] It should have been obvious to the faint-hearted had they noted that, despite creeping protectionism and the slowing down of Northern growth,

whereas in the 1960s LDC exports of manufactures grew

---

32   *Ibid.*
33   Little, Scitovsky, Scott [145], Balassa [11 and 13], Bhagwati [24], Krueger [98].

Table 3 **The structure of LDC exports: selected years, 1955–78, %**

	1955	1960	1970	1978
Total exports	100.0	100.0	100.0	100.0
Food	36.5	33.6	26.5	16.4
Agricultural raw materials	20.5	18.3	10.0	4.8
Minerals, ores	9.9	10.6	12.3	4.6
Fuels	25.2	27.9	32.9	52.8
Manufactures[a]	7.7	9.2	17.7	20.9
Total non-fuel exports	100.0	100.0	100.0	100.0
Food	48.9	46.7	39.5	34.8
Agricultural raw materials	27.4	25.3	14.9	10.1
Minerals, ores	13.3	14.6	18.3	9.7
Manufactures[a]	10.4	12.8	26.4	44.4
Share of DCs in exports of LDCs				
Total non-fuel exports	76.3	74.3	71.9	65.4
Food	79.0	77.7	74.0	65.6
Agricultural raw materials	74.3	67.8	64.4	61.8
Minerals, ores	94.5	92.0	89.2	78.0
Manufactures[1]	45.9	54.0	61.2	63.3

a Manufactures: SITC 5 to 8 less 68.
Source: James Reidl [175], Table 1, p. 18.

> almost twice as fast as DC real GDP ... in the 1970s, despite
> a general slowdown of growth after 1973, LDC exports
> maintained their rapid pace, growing four times as fast as
> DC real GDP.[34]

But protectionism now poses a serious threat to the future growth of LDC exports.

A game with no losers

It is instructive to examine the reasons why protectionism poses a more serious threat to Southern prosperity than the mere slowing

---

34 Reidl [175].

down of Northern growth, since they pinpoint both the real dangers to Third World development in the external environment and the unrealism of the major assumption behind Lewis-type views. These engine-of-growth models cannot explain why developing countries' manufactured exports have been able to grow faster than developed countries' incomes since they implicitly, but falsely, assume there are no domestically-produced substitutes in developed countries to be displaced by the goods developing countries export. They further assume that the supply of developing countries' exports is perfectly elastic so that export volumes will be solely determined by developed countries' expenditure on these goods.

The first assumption, however, does not apply to the manufactured exports of developing countries. They consist of goods like textiles, clothing, footwear and engineering products which compete successfully with manufactures produced by developed countries. By replacing increasingly uncompetitive, import-competing goods in developed country markets, developing countries can expand their manufactured exports even though total incomes, and therefore aggregate demand for manufactures, are stagnant in developed countries. This is precisely how the 'static' law of comparative advantage was supposed to work, with inefficient domestic production being replaced by competitive imports.

But this elimination of some import-competing industries does not imply any justification of the Myrdal-Balogh type of argument about the inimical effects of trade as a 'zero-sum game' – this time to the disadvantage of the North. For the replacement of inefficient lines of production by cheaper imports, apart from the obvious gains it confers on consumers, allows the release of resources for more efficient and productive uses. It is the normal form of economic change which releases resources from relatively unproductive industries where a country's comparative advantage is being eroded for use in relatively more productive activities in line with the country's *emerging* comparative advantage. It should be remembered that a country can be at an absolute disadvantage in terms of productivity in every line of production compared with some other country – or even the rest of the world – and yet it must as a matter of logic have a comparative advantage (or no comparative disadvantage) in terms of *relative* productivity in at least some lines of production. This truth is often ignored in popular discussion of the effects of trade.

The so-called 'static' gains from international trade do not, therefore, depend upon growth in overall incomes in two countries or regions. As a result of the specialisation of production, induced by moving resources from industries with a comparative disadvantage into those with a comparative advantage, the country importing competitive manufactured goods will be able to raise its overall productivity and real income. To resist these changes is to accept lower real incomes and productivity than is necessary. The growing resistance of the North to these desirable shifts in industrial structure is a major reason for the hardening of their economic arteries and thus, in part, for their current slumpflation. But it also poses a danger to the ability of poor countries to develop in line with their own comparative advantage.

Table 4 (p. 84) facilitates a balanced assessment of this danger. It will be seen that, even after the recent spurt in the manufactured exports of developing countries, they still have a minuscule share of the consumption of manufactured goods by developed countries (about 3.4 per cent in 1979). Nevertheless, protectionist lobbies for a small number of industries in developed countries are

arguing that there is a massive Third World challenge. Their demands must be resisted, primarily because of the form of protection they advocate. As in developing countries, the favoured
protective instrument is the quota in whatever euphemistic guise
(for example, 'voluntary' export restraints or managed trade).
Apart from the obvious damage quotas inflict on the well-being of
both workers and consumers in developed countries, they particularly harm the interests of those developing countries (often the
poorest) which are entering the field of manufacturing for export.

Developing and developed countries can be located on a ladder according to their comparative advantage in different manufactured commodities.[35] The 'voluntary' export restraints
increasingly imposed by the developed world are particularly biased against those countries which are just about to climb a particular rung of the ladder. For, as with the allocation of *import* quotas
in developing countries, the distribution of *export* quotas also
tends to reflect 'historic and fair' shares which favour existing exporters at the expense of more efficient newcomers. The biggest
contribution the North can make to the development process,
therefore, is not – as Brandt, Lewis and others argue – to expand
aggregate monetary demand, but rather to eschew the use of quantitative restrictions on imports from the Third World (of which
the Multifibre Arrangement for textiles is the most notorious but
by no means the only example).[36]

---

35 Lary [122] and Lal [112]. For LDC export performance and prospects in the 1960s
    and 1970s, Hughes and Waelbroeck [80]; and Balassa [12] for their prospects in
    the 1980s. Also Blackhurst *et al.* [31].
36 For a detailed analysis of the MFA, Keesing and Wolf [90]. It should be noted,
    however, that it may be easier to resist protectionist pressures if OECD growth is
    resumed.

Table 4 **Share of imports in the consumption of manufactured goods in industrial countries by major product groups, 1970–79, %**

ISIC code	Product group	All imports 1970	Developing country imports 1970	All imports 1979	Developing country imports 1979	— Growth of — import shares All imports 1970–79	Developing country imports 1970–79
31	Food, beverages and tobacco	8.6		10.8	3.9	2.4	2.1
32	Clothing, textiles and leather	11.6	2.7	23.8	9.6	7.8	14.8
33	Wood products	9.5	1.8	16.0	3.8	5.5	7.8
34	Paper and printing	6.6	0.1	8.7	0.4	3.1	13.4
35	Chemicals	10.6	2.0	14.9	3.4	3.1	5.2
36	Non-metallic minerals	5.9	0.3	9.3	1.0	5.0	13.2
37	Metals	15.0	3.2	18.4	3.5	2.2	1.4
38	Machinery	11.3	0.3	21.9	2.0	8.0	21.8
39	Miscellaneous	18.8	8.0	36.6	18.2	7.3	7.2
3	Manufacturing	10.6	1.7	16.8	3.4	5.1	8.1

Source: Helen Hughes and Jean Waelbroeck [80], p. 135.

The terms of trade

It remains to consider the other assumption which underlies the modern variant of the engine-of-growth-type argument – namely, the perfect elasticity of supply of developing countries' exports. For this also is at the root of the new twist recently given to the pessimistic view of the terms of trade of developing countries. The basic hypothesis is that, in developing countries, there are unlimited supplies of labour available at a constant real wage for employment in plantation agriculture or other exporting activities. This hypothesis also underlies a famous model of development, formulated by Sir Arthur Lewis in the 1950s,[37] which has been very influential in seeming to justify both forced industrialisation and pessimism about the effects of so-called 'capitalist growth' in de-

37 Lewis [126].

veloping countries on the incomes and welfare of their poorer members. Its extension to a model of international trade is the work of Lewis and Ronald Findlay.[38] The simplest of these models (attributable to Lewis) is outlined below – not because its predictions are empirically valid but because its apparent plausibility may yet prompt another wave of trade pessimism.

Lewis considered a world divided into two countries, the North and the South. Both produce food and one other good with a single factor of production – labour. The North's other good is manufactures (steel); the South's a primary commodity (coffee). All three goods are consumed and traded by both countries. It is assumed that the North can produce either two units of food or six units of steel with one unit of labour, and that the relative productivity of labour in producing these two goods does not alter as production is switched from producing one good to the other – in other words, that the opportunity cost of labour used in steel production remains constant at two units of food forgone per labourer irrespective of the increase in steel production. The South, too, has fixed labour coefficients in the production of its two commodities, coffee and food. These are one unit of food or nine units of coffee produced by one unit of labour. Since, through arbitrage, the international price of food (which can be taken as the *numéraire* in this 'food theory of value') will be equalised, the international prices of steel and coffee must settle at one steel to three coffee. Changes in the terms of trade will then depend upon relative changes in the respective productivity of labour in the two countries. Thus, if technical progress is faster in Northern food production than in manufacturing, even with

---

38   Lewis [127], Findlay [58].

unchanged Southern productivities the terms of trade will inexorably turn against the South. The only way the South can improve its terms of trade is by raising its productivity in food production relative to coffee at a faster rate than the North raises its productivity in food relative to manufacturing.[39]

Lewis later[40] extended this model to eliminate the dubious assumption of fixed labour productivities. Instead, he argued on historical grounds that virtually the same effects were assured by the North and South having access to two independent sources of unlimited labour at different but constant real wages. The Northern areas of new settlement had access to migrants from the agricultural regions of Europe. The tropical producers of the Caribbean, South-East Asia and other areas of plantation agriculture had access to the pools of low-wage agricultural labourers from China and India. It was the relative productivities of these two streams of migrants in their home agriculture which determined the opportunity cost of labour for the expansion of the export production of the North and South. Since, on Lewis's estimates, the two streams were about the same in the second half of the 19th century (about 50 million migrants each), they set the terms of trade between tropical and temperate exports.

> In the 1880s the wage of a plantation labourer was one
> shilling a day, but the wage of an unskilled construction
> worker in Australia was nine shillings a day. If tea had been
> a temperate instead of a tropical crop, its price would have
> been perhaps four times as high as it was. And if wool had
> been a tropical instead of a temperate crop, it could have

---

39 For a more explicit model, Findlay [58].
40 Lewis [130].

been had for perhaps one fourth of the ruling price. The analysis clearly turns on *the long-run infinite elasticity of the supply of labour to any one activity determined by farm productivity in Europe and Asia, respectively.*[41]

The elastic notion of unequal exchange

Whatever the merits of this view about the determinants of the terms of trade of tropical *vis-à-vis* temperate products in the 19th century, its relevance today is clearly limited because of the inapplicability of the passage in italics which, as Lewis accepts, contains the crucial assumption. Immigration restrictions in both developed and developing countries have considerably reduced the effects of migration from the 'surplus labour' pools of China and India (assuming they still exist). Moreover, it is only in a model with one factor of production – namely, labour – that relative commodity prices will be determined by labour productivity alone, and hence there will be no difference between the commodity and the so-called double factoral terms of trade.[42]

Lewis's second model refers explicitly to the factoral terms of trade and their determinants, since he argues that

the fundamental sense in which the leaders of the less developed world denounce the current international economic order as unjust [is] that the factoral terms of trade

---

41   *Ibid.*, p. 16 (emphasis added).

42   The commodity terms of trade (C) is the ratio of the price index of exports (Px) to that for imports (Pm), that is, $C=Px/Pm$. The double factoral terms of trade (F) are equal to the commodity terms of trade corrected for changes in productivity in the home country's export industry (Zx) and in the foreign industry's supplying the home country's imports (Zm), that is, $F=C.Zx/Zm$.

are based on the market forces of opportunity cost and not on the just principle of equal pay for equal work.[43]

He thus suggests that a productivity gain which reduces the prices of Southern exports would not lead to any Southern gain. This is, of course, the notion of unequal exchange which underlies many neo-Marxist writings. It should be noted, however, that, although movements of the factoral terms of trade may demonstrate to those who believe in a labour theory of value and Marxian notions of exploitation the changing incidence of their notion of justice, the movements are irrelevant in assessing how the welfare (as measured by their real income) of those workers who have suffered a deterioration in their factoral terms of trade will have altered.

Thus let us suppose that, in the simple Lewis world, the South raises the productivity of its labour input into coffee production relative to that into food. The result will be to lower the price of coffee relative to steel by the same proportion, so that the South's factoral and commodity terms of trade deteriorate by the extent of the productivity improvement. It might suggest that the South has derived no benefit from the increased productivity. This is not so, however, if the South also consumes the coffee it produces and exports. For then the productivity increase in coffee will enable the proportion of the labour force producing coffee for domestic consumption to produce more than hitherto. This consumption gain, which can be transferred into any combination of steel, food and coffee (at the new international relative prices of these goods), will not disappear – even though the labour force employed in produc-

---

43   Lewis [130], p. 19.

ing coffee for export succeeds in producing only the same amount of imported steel and food as before.

The objective of judging the desirability of particular trading arrangements by reference to movements in the factoral terms of trade is odd, to say the least. Thus it is easy to construct examples where the so-called double factoral terms of trade of the South worsen but both its commodity terms of trade and the real income of its workers (and of those in the North) increase.[44] This would, however, still be a position of unequal exchange for the neo-Marxists, and therefore undesirable.[45] Perhaps for most workers in the Third World, the only thing worse than being exploited, in this sense, is *not* being exploited!

Findlay has recently produced a most elegant theoretical model to explain a secular tendency for the commodity terms of trade of the South to deteriorate and for its growth rate to be entirely dependent on that in the North, so that trade is inexorably the engine of growth. The crucial assumption in his model is, once again, the unlimited supplies of labour available at a fixed real wage for export production in the South. Reminiscent of the foreign-exchange bottleneck-type views is his further assumption that the South does not produce the capital goods it requires for domestic capital formation and growth and can only acquire them from the North by trading its primary commodity exports. Apart from the dubious empirical validity of both assumptions, the central prediction of his theory that the North will retain its productivity gains whereas the South will export *its* gains through its

---

44 Findlay [58].

45 A. Emmanuel [55]. Samuelson [180] provides a critique of Emmanuel's theory and remarks that 'it is tautologically a restatement of the fact of assumed wage differential'.

deteriorating terms of trade is not borne out by the empirical evidence Findlay himself presents.[46] His model, like those of so many other distinguished predecessors in development economics, is therefore yet another theoretical curiosity!

Dependency theories

In the new wave of counter-attacks against outward-looking trade and payments policies, two others may be noted. The first is by the so-called dependency school, whose prophets are Samir Amin, Andre Gundar Frank, F. H. Cardoso, O. Sunkel, Ranjit Sau, and a host of other Marxist writers.[47] But not all Marxists subscribe to this school. Indeed, the most acute and bitter critics of dependency theories are those who would consider themselves to be on the Left, if not Marxists. It is virtually impossible to give a brief, coherent account of their views for, as one of those critics on the Left has stated:

> The difficulties in criticising Samir Amin's work are severe, mainly because of certain inbuilt immunities which Amin himself has constructed ... These are associated in his work with a mode of argument that takes the form of 'assertion-plus-threat'; i.e., a statement is followed by a 'threat' which applies to those who disagree with the statement. The 'threats' are such accusations as Trotskyism, anarchism or revisionism, economism, Ricardianism, or simply a failure to understand Marxism. The effects of this mode of argument and of these built-in immunities are,

---

46 As noted by the discussant of his paper, S. Grassman, in Grassman and Lundberg [60].

47 An excellent critique of these unorthodox theories is in Little [140]. S. Amin [5] is the major reference for this school.

however, that Amin's analysis is tautological, uninformative and sterile.[48]

The gist of the dependency thesis seems to be that the 'centre' has exploited the 'periphery' for over 400 years, first through 'colonialism' and 'imperialism' and more recently through the neo-colonial form of 'dependent capitalism' it has engendered in the Third World. The exploitation consists of appropriating the 'surplus value' of the Third World; in most versions, the existence of unequal exchange in trade is considered to be a sign of it. Unequal exchange is said to prevail whenever countries whose profit rates have been equalised by the free international flow of capital, but whose real wages differ, trade with each other. The remedy proposed is for the countries of the South to 'de-link' from the North, either by promoting national autarky or, less dramatically, by 'collective self-reliance' through customs unions and other forms of economic integration. Since part of the dependency thesis is that the cultural and political effects of neo-colonialism have warped the minds and hence the attitudes of peoples in the South, de-linking is also expected to lead to a resurgence of national cultures and self-respect.[49]

The premise that an independent (that is, broadly-based and indigenously-propelled) industrial capitalism is not feasible in the Third World has been questioned by Bill Warren amongst others,[50] whilst Sheila Smith has attacked the political wisdom of de-linking from the North:

---

48 Sheila Smith [194], pp. 11–13,

49 Diaz-Alejandro [51], Lal [108].

50 B. Warren [211].

Amin's proposition that only a radical and complete break with the world capitalist system will provide the necessary conditions for genuine development can only be described as dangerous arrogance. The tragic example of Kampuchea may be dismissed as an 'appearance', but the attempt was clearly made in that country to break with the world capitalist system, and with disastrous consequences.[51]

This criticism by no means implies that those Marxist writers who object to dependency theory are thereby reconciled to the 'independent capitalism' they see rampant in the Third World. Their aim is still to replace the capitalist system with a 'socialist' one, *despite* their acceptance that capitalism can lead to a high growth of incomes as well as the alleviation of poverty. For them, capitalism *per se is* abhorrent, irrespective of its fruits. Their abhorrence is presumably moral. Moreover, at least some of them identify 'socialism' with the current practices of Eastern Europe, Cuba and China – that is, with what in normal usage are labelled communist countries. Since true development for these neo-Marxists is 'socialist' development, their argument becomes the tautological one that only the fruits of growth generated by a communist system are truly those of development![52] The more worldly amongst us may, however, be forgiven for attaching less weight to the moral worth of these different labels than to the effectiveness of alternative economic systems in raising growth, alleviating poverty, and also promoting those civil liberties which – at least on the liberal view of the world – are an essential component of the Good Society.

---

51   S. Smith [194], p. 20.
52   For instance, Sanjaya Lall [120] and my review of this work in *Economic Journal*, March 1983.

Free trade and *laissez-faire*

The final set of arguments advanced against the adoption of more liberal trading and payments policies by the Third World are essentially based on a misunderstanding of the modern theory of trade and welfare. Given the spectacular rate and quality of growth of their economics, the so-called 'Gang of Four' – Hong Kong, Singapore, Taiwan and South Korea – have naturally been extensively studied.[53] The mainstream view of the lessons of their experience has been well summarised by Little:

> Except for Hong Kong, very rapid growth began only in the 1960s in each case after a marked change of policy from import substitution to export promotion ... [their] success is almost entirely due to good policies and the ability of the people – scarcely at all to favourable circumstances or a good start.[54]

Of the four, South Korea has a population about the same size as Egypt, and was poorer than Egypt in 1950. Since it is rather typical of other Third World countries, its experience is considered to be particularly relevant. On South Korea, Little concludes:

> The major lesson is that the labour-intensive, export-oriented policies, *which amounted to almost free-trade conditions for exporters*, were the prime cause of an extremely rapid and labour-intensive industrialisation which revolutionised in a decade the lives of more than fifty million people, including the poorest among them.[55]

After quoting this passage in a recent article, Amartya Sen comments:

---

53 For a lucid account of the lessons to be learnt from their experience, Little [137, 138].
54 Little [138], p. 4.
55 *Ibid.*, p. 34 (emphasis added).

> There is indeed much in the experience of 'the four' to cheer Adam Smith, and *the invisible hand would seem to have done a good deal of visible good*. But is this really the 'major lesson' to draw from the experiences of the four? I would now like to argue that this may not be the case.[56]

He goes on to cite instances of government intervention in Korea, such as import controls and export incentives, as a supposed counter to Little's proposition. *But this is mistakenly to identify the argument for free trade with laissez-faire.* Little himself made clear in the published proceedings of the conference at which he made the statements quoted above that he 'had not used the term "free trade" to be synonymous with "*laissez-faire*". In fact, he had never said that "*laissez-faire*" should be adopted'.[57] It is Sen's mistaken *identification* of Little's 'major lesson' about the desirability of *free trade* with Adam Smith's invisible hand of *laissez-faire* which leads him into the wholly spurious argument that, since the Korean government is interventionist, the Korean success story provides no empirical validation of the case for free-trade policies in the Third World.

Nor does the fact of government intervention imply, as Sen seems to suggest, that intervention is on balance *responsible* for Korea's success. Indeed, it could be argued that success has been achieved *despite* intervention. Thus the change in trade policies in the early 1960s from favouring import substitution to broad neutrality between import substitution and exporting – considered to have been a major reason for Korea's subsequent success – entailed the introduction of interventionist export incentives to

---

56 A. K. Sen [191], p. 297 (emphasis added).
57 Little in ILO [84], p. 12.

counteract the effects of import controls which, though undesir-able from their inception, were not (and have not been) entirely re-moved. If the inefficient import controls were to be maintained, export incentives were desirable on second-best welfare grounds to restore a position amounting to a virtual free trade régime for export production. But this does not mean that the import con-trols which made the export incentives necessary were themselves desirable. It would have been best not to have import controls in the first place, that is, no government intervention in foreign trade. To have two sets of intervention, each to neutralise the harm the other would do alone, is hardly a glowing recommenda-tion for government intervention in trade, and certainly not 'the lesson' that can be drawn from the experience of Korea and other East Asian countries.

Furthermore, the broad neutrality in Korea between produc-tion for export and import substitution ended in the mid-1970s, the existing *dirigiste* machine being used to 'guide' domestic pro-duction towards more import substitution in heavy industry and a highly subsidised agriculture. This about-turn has led to both a slackening in the growth rate of income (in 1980, GNP *fell* for the first time in nearly 20 years – by about 6 per cent – after having grown in the late 1960s and early 1970s at annual rates of 10–15 per cent) and a rise in the rate of inflation (from about 15 per cent a year in the early 1970s to nearly 35 per cent in 1980).[58] The new Kor-ean government has had to re-assess the promotion of heavy in-dustry and seems to be reverting to the former policy of maintaining a rough neutrality between the incentives offered to

---

56   A. K. Sen [191], p. 297 (emphasis added).

57   Little in ILO [84], p. 12.

58   K. W. Kim [93].

different branches of industry by restoring the virtual free-trade régime of the earlier period. It should enable Korea to grow in line with its emerging comparative advantage, which lies increasingly in the production of goods using highly-skilled labour though not necessarily much physical capital. Far from confuting the liberal case for free trade, Korea provides one example of how periods of virtual free trade have been accompanied by a high rate of income growth which has been lowered whenever that policy has been departed from.

Conclusion

In conclusion, therefore, none of these more recent attempts to demolish the case for a liberal trading régime in the Third World is convincing. In the 1950s and 1960s, empirical evidence about the relative merits of import substitution and virtual free trade was absent. Hence, there was at least some doubt whether Nurkseian-type views were valid. Since then, the evidence from a large number of countries in different parts of the Third World, covering virtually the whole of the post-World War II period, strongly suggests that the old classical presumption in favour of free trade (except for the so-called terms-of-trade argument for export taxes)[59] is valid for both developing and developed countries, even though the case for *laissez-faire* may have been undermined. This does not, however, mean that free trade provides a panacea for growth. Trade by itself can rarely be the major determinant of growth; internal factors are more important in explaining the wealth of nations. Yet, though free

---

59 Discussed below, pp. 99–101.

trade is not a sufficient condition for growth, it may in many instances be a necessary one. Though it may not be the 'engine', foreign trade remains – in Kravis's splendid phrase – the 'handmaiden of growth'.

There remain two broad areas of debate about the external environment for development which, though of limited importance, have nevertheless had much ink and passion expended on them. They are international commodity agreements and the role of foreign capital, both public and private, in economic development. Each is discussed, rather cursorily, in the next chapter.

3 THE EXTERNAL ENVIRONMENT II: COMMODITIES AND FOREIGN CAPITAL

International commodity agreements

Much has been written about the Third World's desire to establish commodity schemes[1] to stabilise the prices of its primary commodity exports which are supposed to suffer from both high variability and a long-run declining trend. The variability of prices, it is argued, leads to fluctuations in export revenues which make it difficult for countries specialising in primary commodity exports to plan their domestic economies. Empirical studies have failed, however, to find any relationship between the degree of instability of a country's export earnings and the growth rate of its income.[2] Moreover, as Third World exports have become more diversified, this instability has decreased. And the establishment of various compensatory finance schemes (by the IMF and the EEC) to replenish the foreign exchange revenues of countries hurt by unpredictable falls in the prices of their major exports has mitigated the importance of this 'problem' – assuming for the sake of argument that it *is* a problem.[3]

---

1   Henderson and Lal [76], Corden [47], Behrrnan [20].
2   D. Murray [160], C. W. Lawson [123], which also contains references to earlier studies.
3   H. G. Johnson [87], Chapter 5, contains a concise, though dated, account of such schemes.

Following the example of OPEC, emphasis has therefore shifted to various schemes designed to influence the prices of primary commodities in the hope of raising them relative to the prices of manufactures. Such is the main purpose of the buffer stock schemes promoted in the 1970s by the United Nations Conference on Trade and Development (UNCTAD) in its Integrated Programme for Commodities. Unlike past attempts to rig the prices of primary commodities (including oil) through supply restrictions agreed amongst producers, the UNCTAD programme seeks to bring both producers *and* consumers within its ambit – and for good reason. For few commodities are without either substitutes or alternative sources of supply in developed countries. But to make these administered prices stick would also require Northern policing of Southern price fixing of primary commodity exports. It is unlikely that consumers would agree to (*a*) have the prices they must pay fixed against them and (*b*) ensure the higher prices were enforced. Not surprisingly, little has come of this latest attempt at international *dirigisme*.

If there were a way in which the Third World could collectively raise the prices of its primary products, a supporting case could be made out in terms of second-best welfare economics. As it turns out, this is the only exception to free trade that modern theory would accept on *logical* grounds. A country (or group of countries) concerned only with its national interest and facing declining prices for an export good (as the quantity supplied is increased) is in the position of a monopolist and, ideally, should charge a price which maximises its profit from exporting the good. The price will be given by supplying that quantity at which the marginal cost of production is equated with the marginal revenue from export sales. But it is well known that, for a monopolist, the marginal revenue will be less than the price (equal to average revenue) he receives for the sale.

The problem arises because, though the country (or group of countries) taken collectively has monopoly power in export markets, no individual producer within the country does. Each producer will wrongly assume that the price (average revenue) he receives is also the marginal revenue to his country (or group of countries) and seek to produce a quantity which equates the price with his marginal costs of production. The resulting over-supply, in relation to the output which would have been produced had the lower *marginal* revenue been equated with marginal cost, will depress the price of the commodity below its profit-maximising (from a national or international cartel's viewpoint) monopoly price. The optimal policy to counter this is for the country (or group of countries) to levy an export tax on its producers so that the net-of-tax price they receive is equal to the lower *marginal* revenue from exporting rather than the higher *average* revenue given by the world price of the primary commodity.

In addition to optimising the terms of trade of the primary-producing countries, such a system of export taxes would remove one of the major problems which arise when there is monopoly power to be exploited by a large group of producers. For, in order to raise the price of the primary commodity, some restriction of output is obviously required. Most commodity agreements have broken down in the past because of the failure of the participating countries to accept the required control of their supplies. The quotas for individual producing countries, which are usually negotiated as part of a commodity scheme, are often based on political rather than economic considerations. Hence, they are usually found to be unsatisfactory as time passes and circumstances – including the relative costs of production in the various countries – change. The commodity agreements, therefore, soon break down.

If it is feasible to raise the price of a primary commodity by the collective action of producers (which remains doubtful for most commodities), the necessary control of different countries' supplies would best be implemented through a system of national export taxes agreed to by the producing countries.[4] The negotiation of these taxes will, of course, determine the relative shares of the producing countries in world exports. But this should be no more difficult than to negotiate production quotas. Moreover, the tax system will have the advantage of any scheme relying on the price mechanism. It will not freeze the relative structure of supply in world markets, which can still alter as the comparative advantage of the different countries changes.

It is a sign of the intellectual confusion of the times that the diplomats, bureaucrats and politicians from the Third World who have advanced the recent demands for international commodity agreements have been able to see neither the validity of the case they *could* argue nor the instrument which would, if it is feasible, most effectively raise primary commodity prices. The demand for the Integrated Programme for Commodities demonstrates once again the Third World's suspicion of prices and its preference for quantitative controls. The practical relevance of such commodity schemes is, however, likely to be extremely limited, both because of the limited range of commodities it would be feasible to cover and because, as Table 3 shows, the export

---

4   The case for an internationally-agreed system of export taxes is argued in Henderson and Lal [76].

structure of many developing countries is no longer dominated by primary commodities following their success in diversifying their exports during the last two decades.

International capital flows

It is equally odd that the subject of capital inflows into developing countries arouses such strong passions on both sides of the political and geographical divide. For, according to the World Bank's *World Development Report 1982*, 'external finance accounts for only 13 per cent of the total investment in developing countries (or 4 per cent of world savings)'.[5] This includes official capital flows in the form of soft loans and grants as well as private flows in the form of either direct foreign investment or, more recently, portfolio lending by Western commercial banks. The capital formation which has raised the growth rate of income in the Third World in the post-war era has mostly come from domestic resources. Yet external finance is still held, not least by Brandt, to be a major determinant of the prosperity of developing countries. To sort out the fears and misconceptions here, the following presents a brief outline of the ways in which external finance was held by development economists to provide the essential fuel for growth in low-income countries.

The subordinate role of external finance

The rationalisation of the need for massive capital transfers to developing countries was provided in its most extreme form by the

---

5   World Bank [214], p. 3.

foreign-exchange bottleneck-type of view. To recapitulate, this depended on the assumption of rigidities in transforming domestic resources into import substitutes or exports. As a result, a country willing to save enough to achieve a respectable rate of growth of real income would not be able to transform the savings into investment because it would lack the foreign exchange to finance the fixed import requirements of the investment. It has been shown above that there is no empirical support for this view. Hence the argument that external capital flows are required to ease the foreign-exchange bottleneck faced by developing countries is false; there is no such bottleneck – except of a country's own making.

It was also argued, however, that, even for a country fortunate enough to have a healthy balance of payments, foreign capital inflows would still be required to supplement domestic saving which was assumed to be too low and not easily raised to yield rates of investment and of growth of national income considered sufficiently high. Again, the role of foreign capital inflows has been much exaggerated. The argument that poor countries would not be able to raise their rate of saving since their poverty left them too close to the margin of subsistence has also been belied by post-war experience. Thus the World Bank reports that, whereas *gross* domestic savings were 17 per cent of GDP in low-income developing countries in 1960, they had risen to 22 per cent in 1980; the figures for middle-income, oil-importing countries were 19 and 21 per cent respectively.[6] These statistics can be compared with Lewis's estimate that

net domestic savings of the developing countries averaged about 10 per cent a year in the 1960s, which is not very

---

6   *Ibid.*, p. 118.

different from the ratios of Britain or France in the 1860s
when they were already lenders and not borrowers.[7]

Clearly, limitations on the volume of capital available from domestic sources have not been a major constraint on raising the
growth rate of incomes in the Third World. It is the efficiency of
the resulting investment which differentiates the more successful
from the middling performers. The worry expressed in the 1950s
and early 1960s that poor countries would not be able to save
enough to pull themselves up by their bootstraps, and the implicit
confidence that what capital was available would be efficiently
utilised, have both been disproved by experience. India and Korea
are examples. By the end of the 1970s, India had succeeded in raising its domestic savings rate to 20 per cent and Korea to 23 per
cent. The corresponding investment rates were 23 per cent for
India and 31 per cent for Korea. These differences are not as strik-
ing as those in the efficiency with which the resources were used,
which are crudely reflected in the average social return to investment – that is, the increase in income yielded by one unit of investment in the two countries. The social return in India was about
15 per cent in 1958 and 5 per cent in 1968; in Korea, it was 18 per
cent in 1975.[8] Not surprisingly, whilst Indian GDP grew at annual
rates of 3.4 and 3.6 per cent during 1960-70 and 1970-80 respectively, Korean GNP grew nearly three times as fast at annual rates
of 8.6 and 9.5 per cent during the respective periods.

---

7   Lewis [130], p. 43.
8   The returns have been calculated on so-called Little-Mirrlees lines (Chapter 4
     below, pp. 135–6), making rough adjustments for the distortions in relative prices
     due to the trade control system and for the excess of the private cost of industrial
     labour over its social cost. (Lal [116, 107].)

Table 5 **Composition of net capital flows to developing countries, 1960–62 and 1978–80, %**

Net capital flows	1960–62	1978–80
Official development assistance	59	34
Other non-concessional flows, mainly official	7	13
Private non-concessional flows	34	53
Direct investment	20	14
Export credits	7	13
Financial flows	7	26
Total	100	100
Memorandum item		
Total amount (billions of dollars)		
Current prices	9	84
1978 prices	25	76

Source: World Bank [214], p. 29.

This, of course, does not imply that, other things equal, external capital inflows are undesirable for development. The above differences between domestic savings and investment are accounted for by differences in capital inflows. Critics have therefore attacked the quality of the flows and their presumed side-effects on economic development. The strongest passions have been aroused by foreign aid and private foreign investment. As Table 5 shows, these debates have in a sense become academic with the vast explosion of commercial bank lending, which now comprises the major source of external capital for at least the semi-industrialised countries in the Third World. But this new source of external capital has given rise to further fears and anxieties.

Foreign aid

Foreign aid has been criticised from both the Left and the Right for retarding development – on the Left because of the neo-imperialism aid connotes, on the Right because of the likely pauperisation of the populace of those countries which come to depend on international charity.[9] Given the smallness of the sums involved relative to GNP, total investment, or even the government budget in most developing countries, it would be strange if so much evil could flow from so little.[10] The problem lies in the expectations, often highly exaggerated, aroused by the general arguments frequently advanced in favour of foreign aid.

The fundamental case for giving aid is said to be moral, namely, that the rich should help the poor. From this, many Third World spokesmen have sought to infer that there already exists an international society which subscribes to an egalitarian morality from which the *right* of the poor to be aided by the rich can be deduced. Aid is then demanded, as in Western welfare states, as a matter of *right* and not as a charitable handout. Since, however, there is no international society, nor even a commonly-accepted moral standard amongst the different peoples of the world (witness the widespread abrogation in much of the Third World of those civil rights which are an essential component of the moral system evoked to defend the welfare state in the West), no such *right* to aid can be established.[11] Nevertheless, Western societies

---

9   T. Hayter [72], P. Bauer [17].

10 For instance, foreign aid as a percentage of GNP in 1980 for oil-importing LDCs was less than 2 per cent. Some idea of the importance of aid for different countries can be obtained from the following figures of aid to GNP in 1980: 1.6 per cent for India, 6 per cent for Kenya, 18 per cent for Tanzania. However, as professor Bauer has pointed out to me, the importance of aid to the public sector is better measured by the ratio of aid to total tax revenues. These figures for 1980 are 17 per cent for India, 25 per cent for Kenya and 107 per cent for Tanzania.

11 For a fuller discussion and references, Lal [108].

may think it morally right to aid the poor in the world in line with their own moral code.

The poverty which concerns Western taxpayers is that of poor people, not poor nations, and giving money to the latter may have no or little effect on the former. The prime attribute of the jealously guarded sovereignty of nations is that the relationships between a country's government and its people cannot be questioned by outsiders.[12] Thus there is a strict limitation on the ability of donors to ensure that they are helping to alleviate the poverty of the poorest people in Third World countries, rather than directly or indirectly funding some grandiose prestige project on which a government has set its heart. Attempts to tie aid to identifiable investment projects which do have an impact on the poor can be thwarted if these projects would have been undertaken anyway, for the aid can then be used indirectly to finance some other marginal project which may do nothing for the poor.

Given this so-called 'fungibility' of money flowing into a government's coffers, it has been argued that donors can translate their preference for aiding the poor into action only by directly influencing the deployment of all the instruments of government intervention. On this view, the favoured form of aid is to a government's programme as a whole, with the donors exercising some influence on its composition as a *quid pro quo*. If, however, the aid involved is small in relation to the government budget, it is unlikely that the recipient government will accept what it might consider to be gratuitous advice. If the aid flow is large, on the other hand, there is a danger that charges of neo-imperialism will be levied against the donor, or that the recipient government will

---

12   *Ibid.*

come to depend entirely on handouts and start behaving as a pauper. Hence, the leverage donors can exercise to influence the policies of Third World governments through financial assistance is relatively limited. But it is not non-existent. Given the small sums involved, it may, in a number of instances, have done more good than could have been expected.[13]

This is true of both project and programme aid. The major benefit the developing countries derive from the operations of a number of the multilateral aid institutions, such as the World Bank, is the technical assistance built into the process of transferring the aid money to the recipient countries. Though often sound on general economic grounds, their advice is nevertheless resented for political or emotional reasons. In many instances it would not even have been heard, let alone acted upon, had these institutions been unable to provide the recipient governments with a sweetener in the form of financial resources on more favourable terms than were on offer in commercial financial markets. The grant element in the capital transfers classified as official development assistance seems a derisory sum to pay for the opportunity to carry on this form of international dialogue with those responsible for the design and execution of public policies in the Third World. When heeded, the advice has done some good, at the very least in changing the perceptions of bureaucrats and politicians; in some instances it may have had an appreciable effect in making public policies more economically rational.[14]

This modest argument in favour of continuing foreign aid pro-

---

13 Policy reforms in Taiwan, Korea, Sri Lanka and India (in 1966 and more recently) provide examples.

14 For case studies, Healey and Clift [74] and World Bank [215].

grammes is not likely to appeal to crusaders at each end of the political spectrum who either consider external factors as decisive for development or else want to have a decisive say in the evolution of societies of which they are not active members. Nevertheless, aid can be of importance if ideas have an influence on the conduct of public affairs. Sensible economic advice linked to foreign aid may be the least costly way of countering those ideas which still hamper the progress of developing countries. My conclusion, therefore, is that both the Left and the Right have trained their big guns on a target which at worst does little harm and at best can do, and has done, some good in the Third World.

Direct foreign investment

Direct foreign investment (DFI) arouses even stronger passions than foreign aid. The malign as well as the benign effects attributed to DFI are completely disproportionate both to its past and likely future role in Third World development. Historically, DFI has been important in the development of natural (mainly mineral) resources and public utilities in the Third World. These traditional avenues for foreign investment have been steadily blocked by the rise of economic nationalism and the desire of host countries to acquire all the rents from the exploitation of their natural resources. The current conventional wisdom is that public utilities should be in the government sector. DFI is today increasingly found in manufacturing industry where its virtues and vices are seen to stem from the associated attributes it brings of managerial expertise, new technology, and modern marketing methods, including advertising and foreign marketing connections. These strictly economic effects of DFI in manufacturing industry are discussed in the next Chapter. Here it is only necessary to consider the impact of DFI on various national aggregates, such as domestic savings and the balance of payments, as well as its sundry distributional, cultural and political effects.[15]

In the 1960s, statistical demonstrations were provided of the inimical effects of capital inflows (both official aid and DFI) on domestic savings and thence on the growth rate of developing countries.[16] These exercises were soon shown to be spurious since the definition of 'domestic savings' they used, tautologically, required 'domestic savings' to fall whenever there was a capital inflow.[17] But since it is the rate of investment that influences the growth rate, and no evidence was provided that foreign capital inflows reduce domestic investment, no harmful effects can be deduced from this fall in 'domestic savings'.

The next attack was based on estimates of the so-called 'balance-of-payments' effects of DFI flows. These also were shown to be illogical on the ground that the balance-of-payments effects of DFI which, *ex hypothesi*, raises national income and hence is socially desirable, can be whatever a government chooses.[18] For, in a fundamental sense, the balance of payments reflects the difference between domestic output and domestic expenditure. Even if domestic output rises as a result of DFI – which is a good thing – a government can, through fiscal and monetary means, raise domestic expenditure by even more and thus engineer a balance-of-payments deficit – a bad thing! But the 'problem', if there is one, is with the government's fiscal and monetary policies, and not with DFI.

---

15 The following is based on Lal [100, 104, 110, 111].
16 For example, Griffin and Enos [62], Weisskopf [212].
17 Papanek [170], Miksell and Zinser [155], Lal [110].
18 Little [136], Lal [104, 110].

Nor are the harmful *social* effects attributed to DFI persuasive.[19] It is argued that the existing distribution of income in developing countries makes it more profitable to private foreign investors to produce goods which satisfy the wants of the rich rather than the socially more desirable 'needs' of the poor. It is further argued that the obvious remedy – a direct attack on the undesirable distribution of income – is not politically feasible and hence, as a second-best measure, the distribution of *consumption* should be made more equitable by controlling the supply of consumer goods.

This critique is schizophrenic. It assumes that the rich, who are credited with the power to prevent their incomes and hence their consumption from being cut by direct means, would nevertheless acquiesce in the achievement of the same result through the backdoor method of controlling the supply of consumer goods. Moreover, it is not the pattern of consumption that should concern governments but its volume. Even if government was successful in controlling the supply of luxuries, the rich need not reduce their total consumption. The domestic resources diverted to consumption by the rich would not alter; they would merely be embodied in different consumer goods. Finally, the above critique further assumes that a government which lacks the political power to redistribute income could, however, impose an effective and efficient programme of production control. This, to say the least, is implausible.

---

19   Lal [104].

'Appropriate' products and simple technology

The second set of criticisms of DFI on social grounds concerns the quality of the goods it produces and the means it uses to sell them. It is claimed that DFI results in 'inappropriate' products.[20] They are inappropriate partly because they embody higher quality standards than are required to satisfy the needs of Third World consumers and hence waste resources. Soft drinks like Coca-Cola are often cited as an example.

This argument is fallacious. If lower-cost substitutes are available and consumers in developing countries derive no additional satisfaction from the higher quality of the more expensive product, firms seeking to maximise their profits will produce lower-cost and cheaper substitutes. If Third World consumers, however, prefer the higher-quality product, it is not for anyone to say they should be allowed to consume only the cheaper ones of lower quality. A brief stay in the tropical hinterland should provide sufficient evidence that poor Third World consumers who are willing to pay a premium for a bottle of Coca-Cola are less influenced by the fabled power of multinationals to mould their tastes through persuasive advertising than by the unreliability of their local water supplies. Coca-Cola does, after all, provide a guaranteed disease-free potion in tropical countries where the imbibing of liquid refreshment is a basic need and most local substitutes are likely to be contaminated. On the other hand, the advertising of dehydrated baby food in countries where its use with contaminated water can kill babies (another of the horror stories of DFI) does require government regulation or, at least, public provision of information about the relative nutritional merits of breast- and bottle-feeding – particularly

---

20   Stewart [198].

when the quality of local water supplies is uncertain.

If the deleterious effects of DFI are exaggerated by its opponents, so are its beneficial effects by its proponents. As noted above (p. 109), compared with other forms of foreign capital inflows, DFI brings 'extras' in the shape of technology and managerial expertise. Since, however, most developing countries in the early stages of manufacturing are likely to have a comparative advantage in either light consumer goods or the simpler capital goods (like lathes, hammers and other products of light engineering), their need to scale any great technological and managerial heights requiring DFI is doubtful. The technology of textile mills, and even steel mills, is fairly well known and can be readily purchased without having to rely on DFI. Korea, for instance, though it made use of foreign technology, which it bought, and foreign capital, which it borrowed, has made little use of DFI in its spectacular development. Thus, whilst there may be a valid case for more reliance on private enterprise in developing countries (discussed in the next Chapter), it is by no means co-terminous with that for DFI.

Commercial portfolio lending

Commercial bank loans are the third major form of foreign capital inflows into developing countries. From modest beginnings in the mid- to late 1960s, they became the principal source of external capital for LDCs in the 1970s. The portfolio market for long-term bonds issued by LDC governments had been closed since their widespread default in the 1930s and the imposition by the USA of the so-called 'blue sky' law,[21] which forbade US financial inter-

---

21   Lewis [130], p. 49.

mediaries from holding foreign government bonds. The European market was closed by the widespread use of exchange controls in the post-war period – in the UK until 1979!

Thus, the major 19th-century and early 20th-century source of foreign capital for development – portfolio lending from the richer to poorer countries – was blocked to developing countries until fairly recently. Bilateral and multilateral aid flows in the 1950s and 1960s can thus be justified as providing alternatives to the traditional channels of capital to developing countries. However, these forms of capital transfer (aid and DFI) share the disadvantage, in contrast with portfolio lending, of requiring a fairly intimate relationship between the borrower and lender with all the accompanying misunderstandings and politicisation of economics. The old form of portfolio lending was anonymous and apolitical; lenders were only concerned that their interest payments were made on time.

The same American banking regulations which had led to the demise of the old portfolio lending were responsible for the development of the off-shore banking facilities known as the Euro-currency markets. These were based on deposits in banks outside the USA, initially in dollars but later in other currencies also. In the early years, the main depositors were East European countries, but more recently they have been OPEC countries worried about opening deposits in US banks. The lending based on these deposits has become one of the major sources of external capital, at least for the semi-industrialised developing countries and those poorer ones with some readily-exploitable mineral resources. The restoration of a private portfolio capital market to which developing countries have access – albeit with shorter maturities on their loans than was common with the long-term lending during the 19th and early 20th century and with a larger proportion of sovereign (publicly-guaranteed) borrowing – is one of the major beneficent developments in the post-war international economic order. It provides LDCs with a relatively apolitical market for both their reserve placements and their borrowings. Yet there are dark mutterings of the harm this so-called 'unregulated' market can do to both developed and developing countries, and plans for its control are legion. It may be useful briefly to examine these fears in the hope of exorcising them.

Two types of fear about the Euromarkets are common. The first is the danger that simultaneous defaults by some of the larger Third World and East European countries could lead to the collapse of the whole Western banking system. The second is that developing countries have reached the limits of their ability to service their mounting debt and cannot hope to finance their chronic balance-of-payments deficits in the future by further borrowing in commercial markets. Linked to this is the worry that, whilst the Euromarkets have provided access to foreign capital for the richer and better-endowed developing countries, the poorest have been, and will continue to be, left out in the cold since they are considered to be bad credit risks by the commercial banks.

Third World debt in perspective

These fears seem grossly exaggerated for a number of reasons. First, the size of the Third World's external debt and the costs of servicing it (even for the biggest borrowers such as Mexico, Brazil, and Indonesia) have risen in money terms partly as a result of inflation. The total outstanding long-term external debt of all non-oil-producing developing countries grew from $97 billion at the end of 1973 to $505 billion at the end of 1982 (according to the IMF), of which the part owed to private creditors rose from 50 to 58 per cent over the same period. However, relative to the value of their exports of goods and services (whose nominal values also rose in the inflationary 1970s), the debt ratio was 89 per cent in 1973 and 110 per cent in 1982. If this is considered intolerably high, it should be noted that

> around 1910 the Argentine public external debt amounted
> to 184 per cent of her merchandise exports, a figure
> compatible with the excellent credit rating enjoyed by
> Argentina.[22]

Lewis has estimated that the ratio of debt to exports was 1.8 for all developing countries in 1972 compared with ratios in 1913 of around 2.25 for India, Japan and China, 4.8 for Australia, 5.2 for Latin America, and 8.6 for Canada.[23]

Nor does the cost of servicing this debt seem high by historical standards. Two countries in Latin America, Mexico and Brazil, accounted for 56 per cent of the net claims of the banks on non-oil developing countries at the end of 1980. Table 6 shows Bacha and Diaz-Alejandro's estimates of the net financial cost of servicing the debt of non-oil-producing developing countries in Latin America as a percentage of their exports during the post-war period. It should be noted that, in inflationary times, some of the interest charges represent in reality amortisation of the existing debt and not true interest service charges. Even taking the figures at their

---

22   Bacha and Diaz-Alejandro [8].

23   Lewis [130], p. 59.

Table 6 **Net financial-service charges to non-oil Latin America as percentages of exports of goods and services, 1950–79, %**

Period	Interest	Profits[a]	Interest+ profits[b]	Amortisation[c]
1950–54	1.3	5.9	7.2	2.8
1955–59	2.3	5.2	7.5	7.2
1960–64	4.0	6.5	10.5	10.9
1965–69	5.5	8.8	14.3	13.7
1970–73	7.4	7.1	14.5	17.2
1974–76	11.1	5.5	16.6	19.1
1977–79	12.0	6.8	18.9	28.1(d)

a Includes earnings of direct investments by residents of foreign countries net of taxes, whether remitted abroad or reinvested domestically.
b Interest and profits received by Latin American residents are netted from the payments made under these rubrics. For example, interest earned by Latin American central banks on their holdings of international reserves are deducted from interest payments on the external debt.
c Covers amortisation for both private and public debt of more than one year, but data on amortisation of private debt *not* officially guaranteed are shaky for most countries.
d Refers to 1977–78 only.
Source: E L Bacha and F Diaz-Alejandro [8], p. 16.

face value, the 18.95 per cent for Latin American countries in 1977–79 can be compared with the figures for the period 1900–14. Bacha and Diaz-Alejandro report that these ratios were 39 per cent for Argentina, 22 for Australia, and 24 for Canada; and they were only slightly lower for these countries in 1921–29. Since these figures are based on the ratio of merchandise exports, the comparable figure for Latin American countries in 1977–79 would be 24 per cent – about the same as for the 19th-century countries of 'new settlement'. Bacha and Diaz-Alejandro rightly conclude:

> These comparisons emphasise that the increase in LDC profit and interest payments relative to exports registered during the last thirty years, particularly in the fastest

Table 7 **Real cost of Euromarket credit to developing countries**

Year	%
1976	2.3
1977	0.6
1978	−1.3
1979	0.1
1980	1.8
1981–82	8.0

Source: Overseas Development Institute estimates.

> growing LDCs, represents largely a readjustment by
> creditworthy borrowers to an international capital market
> reborn after the catastrophes of the 1930s and 1940s.[24]

There is no theoretically correct ratio of debt or debt service charges to exports or GDP. As long as a borrower can utilise the loan productively to yield a net rate of return equal to at least the interest rate paid, and can convert the domestic resource equivalent into foreign exchange, foreign borrowing need pose no problem. Until the past two years of high interest rates, these real interest costs of borrowing were extremely low (Table 7), and negative in some years. It is difficult to believe there are no investment opportunities in developing countries today which would yield 8 per cent per annum.

What of the problems of converting domestic resources into foreign exchange – the so-called balance-of-payments burden of servicing the foreign debt? This, of course, is just another version of the foreign-exchange bottleneck-type myth and there is nothing in the external environment that has changed to alter the judgement on this issue delivered above. But if the 'new protectionism'

---

24 *Op. cit.*, p. 17.

Table 8 **Statistics for six major borrowers in private capital market**

Country	Output growth 1970–80 %p.a.	Export growth 1970–80 %p.a.	Medium-term debt service ratio 1981[a] %	% bank debt short-term 1981 %	Cash-flow ratio 1982[b] %
Mexico	5.2	13.4	60	42	129
Brazil	8.4	7.5	58	27	122
Venezuela	5.0	-6.7	37	55	95
Thailand	7.2	11.8	17	55	48
Korea	9.5	23.0	16	53	53
Philippines	6.3	7.0	24	53	91

a Interest and principal on medium-term debt in relation to exports of goods and services.
b Interest and principal on all debt in relation to exports of goods and services.
Sources: World Development Report, 1982 [214], World Bank and Overseas Development Institute.

in the North becomes widespread, it will make servicing the foreign debt more difficult. In that sense, the debt problem is linked to the problem of maintaining relatively free trade in the world economy. It should be noted, however, that, in the 1970s, the major borrowers had no difficulty in increasing their export earnings, or putting the borrowings to productive use, as judged by the growth rates of income (Table 8).

There is much obfuscation about access to the Euromarkets for the poorest countries. Some relatively well-managed poor economies, such as India, have been able to borrow; they *chose* not to enter these markets sooner. The 'problem' seems to concern a number of sub-Saharan countries. Once again, however, the reason they have not been able to borrow as much as they wished is the doubt lenders quite rightly harbour of their ability to make productive use of loans. In countries such as Tanzania, this is partly the result of irrational domestic policies which are tenaciously upheld despite a failure recognised by all except those committed to them.[25] In others, such as Uganda, it is because the most elementary conditions for any economic development at all – law and order – are virtually non-existent. Blaming the outside world for domestic sins of omission and commission may be useful to politicians and bureaucrats, but there is no reason for impartial observers to do the same. From the evidence available, my conclusion is that there is no bias against lending to *poor* countries as such; there is, however, quite rightly a bias against lending to countries which are mismanaged, whether rich or poor.[26]

Faults and defaults

So far, we have discussed the long- and medium-term debt of the Third World. In recent years, however, some countries – mainly in Latin America – have obtained substantial short-term credits from commercial banks (Table 8). These are analogous to the overdraft limits banks offer their domestic customers. Just as a domestic client would expect to pay only the interest on his overdraft out of current income, so repayments of principal on these short-term debts are not usually considered part of the annual servicing costs of Third World debt. It was the failure of the commercial banks to 'roll over' their short-term credits to the major Latin American borrowers which precipitated their debt 'crisis' by creating a short-run cash-flow problem for them (Table 8). Perhaps this was an appropriate tactic to persuade countries whose lax domestic financial policies might have created a debt-servicing problem in

---

25   Acharya [1], World Bank [213], Coulson [48].
26   R. O'Brien [169].

the future to put their houses in order. But the short-run liquidity crisis precipitated by the commercial banks is in itself no more a sign of the unsoundness of these countries' past long-term borrowings or their future ability to service them than would be the arbitrary withdrawal of an overdraft facility from an otherwise sound commercial business.

The commercial banks' withdrawal of credit from some of their major borrowers appears to be a belated recognition of the imprudence of some of their past lending. But capital losses from bad debts are part of the normal risks of banking; they do not justify forcing major debtors into illiquidity. Only if the banks believed that the consequent dangers of default and associated bank failures would force Western governments to organise a 'bail-out' of the commercial banks could it be in the latter's interest to precipitate and proclaim a debt crisis.

Is it reasonable to fear a global banking collapse following simultaneous defaults by a number of large sovereign borrowers? Many commentators are playing on the historical memories of the bank failures during the 1930s. They, however, were not the cause of the Great Depression; the cause was the failure of national governments to prevent the collapse of their domestic money supplies. Since most depositors in Western countries are implicitly or explicitly insured, the failure of imprudent banks need have no dire consequences – provided governments do not allow national money supplies to shrink.

As this is written, a whole host of developing countries, including the major Latin American countries, have asked for their debts to be re-scheduled, which is simply a modem euphemism for a default. Poland has been in default in this sense for some time. Yet the world banking system has not collapsed. Individual banks have collapsed, of which the most notable example is the Herstatt Bank. The convention was established during that episode that the national central banks would act as lenders of last resort for their commercial banks and their foreign subsidiaries. This seems to have worked quite well so far, and it is difficult to see why it should not continue to do so in the future. As Sir Arthur Lewis has emphasised:

> Though defaults by borrowers may appear shocking, they were common in the past. The European capital market took such defaults in its stride. It knew that borrowers would have to come back for more money, and could then be made to recognise outstanding obligations before becoming eligible for new borrowing.[27]

Sanctions for bad debtors – and bad creditors

There may, however, be some need for international sanctions against defaults by sovereign borrowers to fulfil another function of the lender of last resort at an international level, namely, sorting out the good from the bad debtors. A number of legislative provisions in the USA automatically activate penalties on defaulting countries.[28] Thus, though foreign lenders to sovereign Third World governments do not have the same legal redress as liquidating the assets of bankrupt private borrowers, the automatic penalties will act as a deterrent. However, in order for an improvident sovereign borrower to be restored to good health in the international capital market, it may be necessary for that coun-

---

27 Lewis [130], p. 49.
28 Eaton and Gersovitz [54] provide a survey of these issues.

try to accept unpalatable changes in its economic policies. The conditionality of IMF stabilisation programmes is of major importance both in helping establish sound macro-economic policies in countries in crisis and in warning others against unsound policies which might land them in the arms of the IMF.

It is therefore in the interest of those LDCs which intend to continue using international capital markets to resist the erosion of the conditionality rule misguidedly advocated by so many Third World lobbyists. For, in the absence of conditionality, credit to many Third World countries could be restricted by bankers concerned that those intending to default would borrow as much as possible, regardless of the costs.

There is no reason to believe that the IMF's 'seal of good housekeeping' requires it to provide concessional lending as well. The acceptance of an IMF programme should unblock private credit lines to those countries with access to the commercial bond market. There may be an argument for providing such countries with foreign aid and technical assistance to remove the distortions in their economies which lead to frequent balance-of-payments crises. But the international agency with both the traditional mandate and the technical capacity to determine and administer such development assistance is the World Bank. There would be little justification for the IMF duplicating its role. By confusing development aid with the remedies required for a financial crisis (precipitated by inappropriate macroeconomic policies), concessional IMF lending would reduce the incentive for countries to avoid getting into a crisis in the first place.

Some commercial bankers, worried by perceived mistakes in their past lending to certain LDCs, are seeking to have their risks underwritten by an international agency. Bank failures would hurt uninsured depositors and shareholders but, so long as the money supply was maintained, would not lead to a depression. It is arguable whether imprudent banks should be bailed out at taxpayers' expense – whether by their national authorities taking over some of the banks' bad debts, or by their channelling extra liquidity through the IMF to debtor countries to prevent the latter from defaulting. To avoid the 'moral hazard' of bail-outs for future lending, it may not be undesirable to permit a few bank failures. OPEC lent its surpluses to the Third World via the Western banking system, and the latter failed to exercise a sufficient degree of prudence in its lending, because both believed Western taxpayers would ultimately bear the risks. As long as the liquidity of the Western banking system is not allowed to collapse and the rising tide of protectionism in the West is stemmed – thus enabling well-managed Third World countries to service their viable debts – some bank failures which disabuse both OPEC and the commercial banks of their dangerous misconception may well be desirable.

Despite the current short-run problems of the world economy, the institutional framework for maintaining the post-war liberal international economic order, though strained, has not been irreparably damaged.[29] The best service the West can give the Third World is to ensure that *this* economic order is not eroded by refusing to surrender to the blandishments of either the Southern *dirigistes* of the New International Economic Order or the Northern advocates of the 'new protectionism'.

---

29 For a discussion of the desirability of open payments systems and unregulated Euromarkets for developing countries, Lal [115].

4 INDUSTRIALISATION AND PLANNING

Introduction

Industrialisation has become identified with development in much of the Third World. Modern industry is seen to be the hallmark of a developed economy. Haunted by memories of colonialism, most Third World élites also consider the lack of an industrial base to be the major reason for their relative lack of power in their dealings with the West. Industrialisation is seen as an essential base both for their self-respect and for waging modern wars, and its promotion as the chief means to overcome that inherent military weakness which led to their subjugation in the past by superior Western arms. In this context, the *dirigiste* example of the Soviet Union is found particularly attractive since it is deemed to show how a weak and poor underdeveloped country industrialised through planning and became a Great Power within the lifetime of one generation.[1] In the 1950s and 1960s, therefore, industrialisation came to be regarded as the major objective, and planning as the means to engineer economic development.

Aside from these questionable nationalist and militarist motives behind the Third World's drive towards industrialisation,

---

1   I have discussed some of the ideas which feed the Third World's *dirigisme* in Lal [108].

there were also good economic reasons to expect industrialisation to be an important part of its process of development. Although a few developing countries are blessed with valuable minerals, or with large reserves of land relative to the size of their current and prospective populations, most Third World people live in countries whose most abundant resource is labour. Labour-intensive industrialisation, as the example of countries of the Far East which are poor in resources other than labour has dramatically shown (South Korea, Taiwan, Hong Kong, Singapore and Japan), offers a way of making use of abundant labour to raise output, productivity and incomes. For most of the populous Third World countries – India, China, Indonesia, Mexico, Brazil – industrialisation is therefore likely to be an integral part of economic development.

The only relevant questions are: Can anything be said about the appropriate form of this industrialisation, and is there anything governments should do to promote it? Some of the resulting debates were dealt with in Chapter 2 since they have been intimately tied in with the issue of protection. In particular, it was seen that the case for forced, import-substituting industrialisation behind high protective walls has been convincingly refuted by both experience and theory. Forced industrialisation has led to both an inefficient use of available resources and arbitrary and inequitable changes in the distribution of incomes. Thus the large sacrifices most Third World people have made in reducing their meagre current consumption to permit massive post-war increases in savings and investment have not been translated into the growth of incomes that was feasible. Nor, in terms of alleviating poverty, has the quality of what growth has been achieved been as good as it could have, judging by the performance of other countries which did not attempt to force import-substituting industrialisation beyond the size and form dictated by their comparative advantage – which both theory and experience tell us is best promoted through maintaining a régime of virtual free trade.

The promotion of industry

Does this conclusion imply, as some have argued, that an industrial policy close to *laissez-faire* is appropriate? Chapter 1 offered reasons why, *prima facie,* such an implication is not tenable. The ubiquity of increasing returns and external effects in industrial production is usually cited in favour of government intervention,[2] whilst the absence of entrepreneurship or a desire to prevent the concentration of economic power in a few private hands is taken to require the more direct involvement of governments to establish state-owned industrial enterprises.[3]

In addition, there are the old-fashioned or more traditional tasks of government in promoting industrialisation. The most important are to establish and maintain the country's infrastructure. 'Non-traded' services such as roads, communication systems (like telephones) and other utilities (like the electricity essential for industrialisation) all require large, indivisible lumps of capital before any output can be produced. Since they also frequently have the characteristics of public goods, natural monopolies would emerge if they were privately produced. Some form of government regulation would be required to ensure the services were provided in adequate quantities at prices which reflected their real resource costs. Government intervention is therefore necessary. And, given

---

2   By Scitovsky [184] and Hirschman [78] among others.

3   For a discussion of the arguments for and against public enterprises, Lal [117].

the costs of regulation in terms of acquiring the relevant information, it may be second-best to supply the infrastructure services publicly. These factors justify one of the most important roles for government in the development process. It can be argued that the very large increase in infrastructure investment, coupled with higher savings rates, provides the major explanation of the marked expansion in the economic growth rates of most Third World countries during the post-war period, compared with both their own previous performance and that of today's developed countries during their emergence from underdevelopment.

On planning

It became one of the canons of development economics that much more was required of governments to promote industrialisation. Planning was the panacea on offer. Although, in practice, it has come to have as many variants as adherents, planning has usually been identified with the form of government intervention employed in the Soviet Union or the People's Republic of China. Its principal feature is the central determination of the physical *quantities* of the goods and services which are the inputs and outputs of the myriad industries which make up the so-called 'industrial sector'.[4] It is an attempt to supplant the working of a market economy. Its economic rationale must depend upon the considerations derived from welfare economics outlined in Chapter 1.

These issues were aired in a famous debate between Oskar Lange, Abba Lerner, Ludwig von Mises and Friedrich Hayek during the 1930s and 1940s.[5] The planners (Lange and Lerner) argued

4   For a fuller discussion of alternative forms of planning, Part I of Lal [116].

5   Lange [121], Lerner [125], Hayek [71], von Mises [156].

(*a*) that, because of the ubiquitous imperfections in most markets, no market economy could ever in practice attain the utopian norm of perfect competition, and (*b*) that, by using computers to simulate the outcome of a perfectly competitive economy and legislating to compel the production of the resulting quantities of inputs and outputs (or their relative prices), a planned economy could achieve Utopia. Hayek and Mises pointed out that, though such a form of planning might be theoretically feasible in a world where information about resources, technology and the myriad actual and possible production processes and tastes of consumers could be costlessly acquired by the central planning authority, in the real world it would be impossible. Moreover, even if it were possible to acquire the information, it would be impossible speedily to solve the resulting system of millions of simultaneous equations.

Experience with planned economics, particularly that of the Soviet Union, provided factual corroboration of the Mises-Hayek position.[6] Economic theorists[7] soon demonstrated that, whilst the planners might acquire the relevant information by, in effect, playing a game with *truthful* producers which elicited their profit-maximising combinations of inputs and outputs at different (hypothetical) relative prices, the game would converge to a unique and optimal outcome only if the technological conditions were identical with those required for a market economy to be perfectly competitive. That this should be so is not surprising since the planners are envisaged as playing a game identical to that played by the so-called 'Walrasian auctioneer' in a perfectly-competitive economy. But if the real world conformed

---

6   Nove [165].

7   Heal [73] surveys this literature.

to the technological assumptions of the perfect competition model, we would observe perfect competition in a market economy and the planners would be redundant! Conversely, if the technological features of the real world are such that perfect competition cannot exist, omnipotent but *not* omniscient planners will be unable to simulate such a condition in a planned economy.

Further, there can be no assurance that the producers tell the truth; it may be in their interest to lie systematically to the planners in order to obtain, for example, a larger share of inputs (say, leather) to produce the planned output (say, shoes). In this instance, even if the world met the technological requirements for perfect competition, because of this so-called 'incentive incompatibility' the planned economy would not attain Utopia – whereas, by utilising the universal human incentive of self-interest (or greed, as it is emotively labelled), a market economy could.

Foretelling the future

These seemingly unworldly theoretical debates pinpoint the major intellectual assumption underlying the *Dirigiste Dogma*, as well as its obvious limitations. Behind most arguments for government intervention, particularly those based on directly controlling quantities of goods demanded and supplied, is the implicit premise of an omniscient central authority. Furthermore, to achieve Utopia the authority must also be omnipotent (to prevent people from taking actions which controvert its diktat) and benevolent (to ensure it serves the common weal rather than its own). Whilst most people are willing to question the omnipotence or benevolence of governments, there is a big temptation to endow the latter with an omniscience which private agents know they themselves lack. This temptation is particularly big when it comes to foretelling the future.

Nearly all investment involves giving hostages to fortune. Most investments yield their fruits over time and the expectations of investors at the moment they are made may not be fulfilled. Planners attempting to direct industrial investments and outputs have to take a view about future changes in prices, tastes, resources and technology, just as private individuals do. Even if the planners can acquire the necessary information about *current* tastes, technology and resources in designing an investment programme, they must also take a view about likely changes in the *future* demand and supply of a myriad of goods. Because in an uncertain world there can be no agreed or objective way of deciding whether a particular investment gamble is sounder than another, the planned outcomes will be 'better' than those of a market system (in the sense of lower excess demand for or supply of different goods and services) only if the planners' forecasts are more accurate than the decentralised forecasts made by the mass of individual decision-makers in a market economy. There is no reason to believe that planners, lacking perfect foresight, will be more successful at foretelling the future than ordinary mortals.

Outcomes deriving from centralised forecasts may, indeed, turn out to be worse than those based on the decentralised forecasts of a large number of participants in a market economy because imposing a single centralised forecast on the economy in an uncertain world is like putting all eggs in one basket. By contrast, the multitude of small bets, based on different forecasts, placed by a large number of decision-makers in a market economy may be a sounder gambling strategy. This assumes, of course, that the government does not have more information about the future than private agents. If it does, it should obviously disseminate it, together with any of its own forecasts. On the whole, however, it may be best to leave private individual decision-makers to gamble according to their own judgements.

This conclusion is strengthened by the fact, emphasised by Hayek, that most relevant information is likely to be held at the level of the individual firm and the household. A major role of the price mechanism in a market economy is to transmit this information to all interested parties. The type of 'planning without prices' favoured by most planners attempts to supersede and suppress the price mechanism. It thereby throws sand into one of the most useful and relatively low-cost social mechanisms for transmitting information, as well as for co-ordinating the actions of a myriad of interdependent market participants. The strongest argument against centralised planning of the Soviet or Maoist variety, therefore, is that, whilst *omniscient planners* might forecast the future more accurately than myopic private agents, there is no reason to believe that flesh-and-blood bureaucrats can do any better – and some reason to believe they may do much worse.

Picking industrial 'winners'

It has nevertheless been maintained that planners in the Third World can and should directly control the pattern of industrialisation. Some have put their faith in so-called mathematical programming models based on the use of input-output tables developed by Leontief.[8] But, partly for the reasons just discussed, little reliance can be placed upon either the realism or the useful-

---

8   Above, p. 45, and [124].

ness of these models for deciding which industries will be 'losers' and which will be 'winners' in the future. More seriously, all the difficulties in obtaining the information required to describe the existing technological choices at the level of an individual industry are present in the derivation of an input-output table. Even at their best, these summarise the existing choices which have been made in an economy of very broadly-defined inputs and outputs of fairly highly aggregated categories of 'industries'.

As a snapshot description of the technology of production, the tables can never provide a completely disaggregated picture of the inputs and outputs at the relevant level – the level required, for instance, for knowing what inputs go into producing nails, or fasteners, or bicycle wheels, or any of the other myriad goods produced in a real-world economy. Nor can they reveal the whole spectrum of technological choices at the level of an actual industry since they merely report *particular* choices made in a given economic environment at a certain date, and there is no reason to believe those choices will be appropriate in all circumstances. It is also far from easy to keep the tables up to date, even as a relatively aggregative description of the economy.

An example can be cited from India – a country which has made serious efforts to implement Soviet-style planning in its industrial sector. Whilst working for the Indian Planning Commission in 1974, the author sought to provide a crude estimate of the likely direct and indirect demand for oil resulting from different rates of growth of GDR. With the development of the indigenous fertiliser industry, one of the more important uses of oil was in producing fertilisers. The available input-output table led to a gross under-estimate of the direct and indirect demand for oil generation by agriculture because the oil input into fertiliser production was based on data obtained at a time when India had no oil-based fertiliser plants!

It would be pointless to cite the various irrationalities of industrial policy which planning without prices in India and many other countries has entailed.[9] If, however, planning is identified with the design of rational government intervention, more acceptable forms of planning can be envisaged. These essentially involve: identifying distortions in the working of the market economy; identifying the various instruments of public policy which can be used to deal with the distortions; and ranking the instruments according to their net effects on economic welfare, taking into account the costs of acquiring the information necessary to deploy a particular instrument plus those resulting from any new distortions the instrument itself may create.

This exercise in applied welfare economics – which is all that 'rational' planning amounts to – may reveal that *none* of the feasible instruments of policy allows a *net* improvement in welfare compared with the market outcome. From the experience of a large number of developing countries in the post-war period, it would be a fair professional judgement that most government interventions attempting to supplant the price mechanism (by direct controls) have done more harm than good – even compared, possibly, with *laissez-faire*. Most of the more serious distortions in the current workings of the price mechanism in Third World countries are due not to the inherent imperfections of the market mechanism but to irrational government interventions, of which foreign trade controls, industrial licensing, and various forms of price control are the most important. In seeking to improve upon

---

9   For India, Bhagwati and Desai [25], and Lal [116].

the outcomes of an imperfect market economy, the *dirigisme* to which numerous development economists have lent intellectual support has led to so-called 'policy-induced' distortions which are more serious than any of the supposed distortions of the imperfect market economy it was designed to cure.

Social cost-benefit analysis

One of the major intellectual advances both in diagnosing the policy-induced distortions and in pointing the second-best way towards their removal has been in what is called 'social cost-benefit analysis' – an application of second-best welfare economics which has been developed with the problems of Third World countries in mind. The most famous of the various methods of cost-benefit analysis, that devised by Little and Mirrlees, is based on the important theoretical insight that in many second-best situations the pursuit of full-blooded economic efficiency may lead to the second-best optimum. This considerably simplifies the task of appraising and designing public policies for an imperfect economy.[10]

Consider a simplified example. Assume a country whose economy produces only two goods – say, cloth and food – both of which can be traded internationally at constant and fixed prices (terms of trade). Cloth is also imported and food is exported. For some reason, the country has imposed a tariff on the import of cloth so that its domestic production of cloth has expanded relative to that of food, compared with what the situation would have been under free trade. Let us suppose further that the government

---

10   For a simple account of the logic of these procedures, Little and Mirrlees [143], Lal [103].

will not remove the tariff in the future. The question to be asked is: Should any incremental resources be invested in expanding the domestic output of cloth or food? At the ruling, tariff-inclusive prices of cloth and food, the production of both goods is equally profitable. It can be shown, however, that economic welfare is increased if the choice of investment is made not at the distorted, tariff-inclusive prices, but at the net-of-tariff (or world) prices of the goods – that is, *as if* the prices under free trade ruled.

This does not mean that free trade *will* rule. Protection continues, but it is still second-best to choose those investment projects which would be chosen if free trade ruled. The prevailing world prices of goods and services provide a set of what are called 'shadow prices', reflecting the relative social (rather than private) costs and benefits of using and producing different goods and services. The shadow prices can be used to make investment and production decisions in the public sector, or to design various rational forms of government intervention without the planners having to acquire the detailed knowledge of underlying demand and supply schedules for a myriad of goods – as they do under the Stalinist or Maoist varieties of planning, including their more sophisticated variants such as mathematical programming models. Of course, in the example cited it may be best of all to remove the policy-induced distortion – the tariff – and thus convert the shadow prices into actual market prices.

The so-called shadow-pricing rules are slightly more complicated in more realistic situations. The derivation of shadow prices, however, and their application in social cost-benefit analyses – not merely to investment projects in the public sector but to the whole gamut of government intervention in the economy, including taxes, subsidies, and direct controls on prices and/or outputs –

provides the only logical basis for rational government intervention. As such, *dirigistes* might have been expected to applaud these theoretical developments and rush to apply them in practice. Instead, misunderstandings and misrepresentation of social-cost benefit procedures abound.[11] In part, this is because of the inherent suspicion *dirigistes* have of any form of intervention which attempts to supplement rather than supplant the price mechanism, as well as their impatience with welfare economics.[12] Equally important, however, is that the application of second-best welfare economics is a complex and delicate intellectual pursuit and, for this reason alone, rational government intervention can rarely be expected in countries which lack expertise within their governments to understand and apply the methods. In such circumstances, the *laissez-faire* outcomes of an imperfect market economy may turn out better than the irrational government interventions which alone are feasible.

Some industrial strategies

For many *dirigistes*, the above discussion will seem to be missing the point. On their view, more is required from governments than 'getting the prices right'. They stress other aspects, not supposedly taken into account by conventional economics, which include such 'values' as technological independence, industrial self-reliance, and the promotion of appropriate technologies and products. The first two of these are supposed to be subserved by

---

11 For instance, Stewart and Streeten [200] and the reply by Little and Mirrlees [144].

12 Streeten and Lall [206], pp. 49 ff. For a critique of their views, Lal [111].

the development of basic or heavy industries, such as cement, steel, petrochemicals, and heavy machinery (machines to make machines). The common feature of most basic industries is that they are very capital-intensive, and encouraging them will often conflict with the third 'value' – appropriate technology – which is quite rightly advocated for most developing countries but which is labour-intensive. The intention seems to be to promote industrial autarky, with the government choosing the appropriate (labour-intensive) technique of production of everything from steel mills to grain production, as well as determining the products to be produced and consumed according to its judgement of 'need'.[13] We have already questioned the feasibility of deriving such a *dirigiste* programme on the ground of the limited information available to any real-world government having to make the myriad choices of individual goods and services. But the *desirability* of such a programme, even if it were feasible, is equally questionable.

Promoting heavy industry

Among Marxists and others on the Left, industrial self-reliance through the promotion of heavy industry has become a *sine qua non* of development. Moreover, a theoretical justification was provided, first, by the Soviet economist Feldman (the intellectual father of the Soviet form of industrialisation who was, however, shot by Stalin for his pains) and later – and independently – by Mahalanobis in India (who was amply rewarded by Nehru for his *ex post*

---

13   This point has been explicitly stated by Sanjaya Lall [120]; cf. D. Lal, *Economic Journal*, March 1983. p. 242.

rationalisation of a policy seemingly forced on India by the foreign-exchange crisis of the early 1950s). Feldman and Mahalanobis[14] showed that the only way for a country in a foreign-exchange bottleneck to raise and sustain consumption levels in the long run was to produce all the goods it physically could which would otherwise have been imported. This was the case of the Soviet Union, which was forced into autarky by trade sanctions and which had a large domestic market as well as a diversified natural base.

Thus, let us suppose that a country produces corn with domestic labour and imports tractors, and pays for the tractors with the foreign exchange earnings from corn exports. The tractors cannot be substituted by any other input into corn production. Let us further assume that the country is unable to raise its foreign-exchange earnings from corn exports above a fixed amount because the foreign demand for its exports is completely inelastic. It faces a foreign-exchange bottleneck. Then, even if it is willing to save more corn (which it wants to use as seed and to exchange through foreign trade for the imported input into corn production – tractors), it will be unable to do so: because of the limited foreign demand for its exports it cannot convert its incremental savings into the foreign exchange required to import the extra tractors.

It was argued that the country could break out of this bottleneck if, instead of using its limited foreign exchange to import tractors, it devoted a major part of it to import machines to make tractors. This would mean that, in the short run, its corn output and hence consumption would fall since there would be fewer tractors available for corn production (as compared with the situation

---

14   The Feldman–Mahalanobis model is clearly explained in Bronfrenbrenner [36].

where only tractors were being imported). In time, however, as the machines producing domestic tractors began to bear fruit, the constraint imposed on the domestic availability of tractors by the fixed foreign-exchange earnings would be removed and corn output and consumption could begin to rise above the amounts set by the foreign-exchange bottleneck. Nevertheless, the domestic supply of tractors would still be limited by the fixed imports of machines to make tractors which the fixed foreign-exchange earnings allowed. Why not then, it was argued, use the fixed foreign exchange in the first instance to import 'grandmother' machines to make the machines to make tractors ... and so on back in the chain of production until the fixed foreign exchange is used to import only the essential raw materials required for products which are not domestically available? In the long run, such a policy would remove all foreign limitations on raising domestic consumption levels – though in the interim, while the chain from 'great-great- ... grandmother' machines to tractors was being put in place, domestic consumption would have to be drastically curtailed, as Stalin's subjects discovered to their cost.

Although, as stated, this argument may appear unreal, it has been the basis of much of the *dirigiste* case for heavy industry in developing countries. Its irrelevance should be obvious from our discussion in Chapter 2, for its central assumption that developing countries are in a foreign-exchange bottleneck is invalid. If the assumption of fixed or stagnant export earnings is removed, the orthodox economic case for an international division of labour and the specialisation of production according to countries' comparative advantage as the best way to raise living standards becomes incontrovertible. Perceiving this, as well as the dismal results obtained in countries like India from attempts to promote industrialisation biased towards heavy industry, *dirigistes* changed their tack in the 1960s from seeking to justify this essentially irrational and ideological predilection for heavy industry.

They now argued that the development of a *capital goods* industry was desirable because it would make it easier to evolve labour-intensive technology more appropriate to the abundance of labour, relative to capital, characteristic of most developing countries.[15] As Little has pointed out,[16] however, there is a distinction between heavy industry and capital goods, which this argument tends to ignore. Capital goods consist of many labour-intensive goods, such as hammers, lathes and pumps, whereas many of the products of heavy industry, such as cement, fertilisers and steel, are intermediate, but not capital, goods. The latter tend to be the products of the engineering industry and many of them are intensive in the use of labour (unskilled and skilled) but not in the use of capital. It is quite likely that many developing countries have a comparative advantage in producing them and that there is no need to promote them especially by *dirigisme*.[17] There is no reason to doubt that, for large countries such as India with varied natural resources, some heavy-industry products, such as steel, would pass a social-cost benefit test of economic desirability. What is irrational is the *dirigiste* claim that there are *general* grounds for preferring one branch or type of industry over another which the government can readily discern by intuition.

---

15 Stewart [199].

16 Little [140].

17 A list of goods in which developing countries are likely to have a comparative advantage is provided by Hal Lary [122].

Controlling transnational companies

Dirigisme is also defended on the ground of controlling transnational corporations. The claim is that DFI must be controlled because its operations are otherwise likely to damage economic welfare in the host country. Studies have attempted to evaluate the social costs and benefits of DFI in a variety of countries.[18] Their conclusion is that all the features generally attributed to DFI (that it is more capital-intensive, invariably produces inappropriate products, makes higher profits than local enterprises, etc.) cannot be established empirically. What does emerge is that, in manufacturing (the sector where DFI is increasingly found and sought by host countries), the degree of effective protection offered to the foreign investor is both the major incentive for foreign investment and the major determinant of the net gain to the host country from his operations. The higher is the effective protection offered, the more likely are social losses to the host country from the operation of DFI.

This conclusion again suggests, in line with common sense, that there is nothing in DFI generically harmful to the economic health of developing countries. It is the domestic – particularly protective – policies they adopt which can make it harmful.

Indian industrialisation in historical perspective

The reader may still harbour some lingering doubts about the case for a free foreign-trade régime, with some government promotion of industry through the provision of an adequate infrastructure (which includes the means for training people in the skills re-

18   Reuber *et al.* [176], Lal [104, 111], Streeten and Lall [206], Vernon [209].

quired for industrialisation) and perhaps some general subsidy of roughly 15–20 per cent to industry in general in those countries where, for various reasons, the private cost of labour exceeds its social cost. It might be argued that such a régime corresponds to what was supposed to exist in the mid- and late 19th century when the Third World failed, however, to industrialise. The historical experience of industrialisation in India is often cited as an example of stunted development during the colonial *laissez-faire* period, in contrast with the post-Independence promotion of a large and diversified industrial base through a network of the most *dirigiste* industrial policies outside the Communist world. Most of these historical perceptions, however, are the product of influential nationalist and Marxist writings whose empirical basis has been questioned by recent research.[19]

Balogh succinctly expresses the popular view of the effects of 19th-century free trade and *laissez-faire* on the development of Indian industry:

> The destruction of the large and prosperous Indian cotton industry by Britain without any compensating long-run advantage to India simply cannot be explained in these terms: it is altogether different from an event such as the end of the silk industry in Coventry. In the latter case there was compensating expansion. In the former case there was not.[20]

There is little doubt that the introduction of cheap Lancashire textiles between 1812 and 1830 destroyed the Indian export trade in cotton textiles which, according to estimates by Maddison, had

19 For references and a fuller discussion, Lal [119].
20 Balogh [14], p. 11.

amounted to about 1.5 per cent of national income in 17th-century Moghul India.[21] From the 1850s, however, with the establishment of a modern industry using Indian entrepreneurship and capital, manufactured cotton exports began to expand. With the subsequent development of the jute textile industry, about 20 per cent of Indian exports were of modern manufactured goods by 1913. Total exports by this date amounted to 10.7 per cent of national income; and thus the growth of manufactured exports from India during the *laissez-faire* and free trade period was quite impressive. It was the growth rate of agricultural exports which was disappointing in comparison with other Asian countries, particularly Japan. Whilst aggregate exports grew by 3 per cent a year between 1883 and 1913, agricultural exports grew at an annual rate of only 1.4 per cent. Japan's agricultural exports grew at an annual rate of over 4 per cent during the same period.[22]

19th-century de-industrialisation in India – thesis refuted

Nor was this period of *laissez-faire* and free trade one of de-industrialisation, as many nationalist and Marxist writers have asserted. Whilst it is likely that some handloom workers were displaced, the claim that the share of industrial employment (in both the handicraft and modern sectors) in total employment declined in the second half of the 19th century is not supported by the available evidence.[23] There was probably, *at worst*, a relative decline in employment in the traditional handicraft sector, as is

21 Maddison [147], p. 55.

22 Lidman and Domerese [132] and Lewis [130].

23 Thorner and Thorner [207], Krishnamurty [96]. Bagchi [10] has resurrected the de-industrialisation thesis, but not convincingly: Kumar and Krishnamurty [99].

borne out by the fact that handloom production remains a substantial industry in India. It would be incredible if, accepting the de-industrialisation thesis, the current size of the handloom industry (supposedly destroyed in the 1820s) were to be explained as the result of government promotion since Independence in 1947!

The growth of modern industry was not, moreover, confined to cotton textiles during the second half of the 19th century. The first jute mill was set up in 1854, only three years after the first cotton mill, and the first steel mill was established by the Tatas in 1911. Other industries, including paper, sugar and engineering, were also established during the free-trade and *laissez-faire* period. The overall rate of industrial growth was higher in India (4–5 per cent a year between 1880 and 1914) than in most other tropical countries, and also exceeded that of Germany (4 per cent). As Lidman and Domerese have observed:

> An index of industrial production based on six large-scale manufacturing industries more than doubled from 1896 to 1914. By 1914 the Indian economy had developed the world's fourth largest cotton textile industry and the second largest jute manufacturing industry.[24]

The industrial development encompassed both import-substituting and export-oriented industries.

Could industrial development have been even faster, or was it hindered by free trade and *laissez-faire?* That industrial promotion may have been required follows from the arguments against *laissez-faire* advanced in Chapter 1. Industrial development was not more rapid in large part because industrial investment was

---

24   Lidman and Domerese, *op. cit.*, pp. 320–1.

highly risky in India.[25] The risks stemmed from the deficiency of the industrial infrastructure, the scarcity of industrial skills in the labour force, and the relative underdevelopment of local credit systems. Public action on these fronts could have reduced some of the uncertainty surrounding industrial investment to ensure that its private return conformed more to the social return.

But was protection also required? Many argued that it was,[26] and, largely for reasons of fiscal expediency, the colonial government gradually introduced a system of discriminating protection after World War I. A rough comparison can be made of the performance of Indian industry in the broadly free-trade period of 1900–13 (for which data are available) with the protectionist period of 1919–39. It shows that, even judging by crude and inadequate criteria such as the rate of growth of manufacturing output, employment and investment, the performance during the free-trade period was better.[27] Of the industries that were growing in the protectionist period, a proper evaluation of the social return to investment is only available for sugar. This shows that such investment was socially unprofitable.[28] Industrial employment grew twice as fast during the free-trade as during the protectionist period. Though the investment *rate* did not rise, the increase in the volume of investment, combined with a slower expansion of industrial employment, meant a rise in the capital intensity of industrial production. If the whole period of protection from 1913 until the present is taken, there has been an accelerating trend in the capital employed in industry and a decelerating trend in the

25 Morris D. Morris [159], and Ray [174].
26 Especially nationalists such as R. C. Dutt [53]. This is also the theme of Bagchi [9].
27 Little [141].
28 Lal [102].

labour employed. Since Independence, a decelerating trend has also developed in industrial output.[29]

Discriminating protection damaging to Indian textile industry

These facts are not surprising because independent India has merely accentuated trends in industrial policy which were set by the introduction of discriminating protection after World War I. Instead of promoting infant industries, much of this protection shielded established ones against technical change elsewhere (cotton textiles against Japanese imports) or fostered industries (such as sugar) in which India had no long-run comparative advantage. The ensuing waste of resources imposed lower growth in both employment and industrial output than was feasible. The fortunes of the Indian textile industry, which under *laissez-faire* and free trade had so triumphantly turned the tables against Lancashire in the second half of the 19th century, provide one of the best cautionary tales to illustrate the central message of this paper.

Part of the troubles of the Indian textile industry arose from the introduction in 1881 – soon after similar rights had been granted to workers in Britain – of legislation to protect industrial labour from perceived abuses. The first of these factory acts was aptly described as 'the result of agitation [in the UK] by "ignorant English philanthropists and grasping English manufacturers"'.[30] As is usual in such alliances, the selfish English protectionist interest *was* better served by this legislation than the altruism of the

---

29   Lal [119], pp. 391–400.
30   Bhattacharya [28], p. 171.

philanthropists. This point is worth bearing in mind at the present time when a similar pauper-labour argument is being resurrected to force Third World governments to grant their labour the same rights, including a common worldwide minimum wage, as those accorded to workers in OECD countries.[31] The protectionist objective, then as now, is to raise the effective price of labour, the most abundant factor of production, on which the competitiveness of a developing country's manufactured exports depends. The rights granted to Indian labour in 1881 hobbled the Indian textile industry in competing for export, and later domestic, markets with the rising industry of Japan. Lower Indian wages reflected lower efficiency. Whereas the Japanese textile industry was built on using female labour working two shifts a day, the Bombay textile industry was hamstrung by labour laws which forbade such long working hours.[32] Indian textile producers demanded protection and got it. The large home market, which provided an easy life as it was increasingly protected from imports, gave little incentive for Indian producers to raise efficiency.

In the post-Independence period, investment in the cotton textile industry was discouraged by the system of industrial licensing set up to achieve the planned pattern of production and investment. The planners deemed existing capacity to be sufficient to meet home demand; and, given their pessimistic assumptions about export prospects, investments to produce for export were discouraged. As a result, India, which had established the first cotton textile industry in the developing world, lost out in the markets for textiles and clothing in North America and Europe which

---

31 Lal [118].

32 Ray [174], p. 67.

boomed in the post-World War II decades. The opportunity India lost was seized by the young upstarts on the Pacific rim – Hong Kong, South Korea and Taiwan – who used the opportunities provided by the supposedly defunct export markets of the industrialised West to transform the living conditions of their peoples within a decade to levels which, for the mass of Indians, still lie at the end of the rainbow.

5 POVERTY, INEQUALITY AND EMPLOYMENT

Egalitarianism is never far from the surface in most arguments supporting the *Dirigiste Dogma*. This is not surprising since, as noted in Chapter 1, there may be good theoretical reasons for government intervention, even in a perfectly-functioning market economy, to legislate for a distribution of income desired on ethical grounds. Since the distribution resulting from market processes will depend upon the initial distribution of assets (land, capital, skills, and labour) of individuals and households, the desired distribution could, in principle, be attained either by re-distributing the assets or by introducing lump-sum taxes and subsidies to achieve the desired result. Once again, if lump-sum taxes and subsidies cannot be used in practice, the costs of distortion from using other fiscal devices (such as the income tax which distorts the individual's choice between income and leisure) will have to be set against the benefits from any gain in equity. This is as much as theory can tell us, and it is fairly uncontroversial.

Ethics

Problems arise because we lack a consensus about the ethical system for judging the desirability of a particular distribution of income. Even within Western ethical beliefs, the shallow utilitarianism which underlies many economists' views about the

'just' distribution of income and assets is not universally accepted.[1] The possibility that all the variegated peoples of the world
are utilitarians is fairly remote! Yet the moral fervour underlying
many economic prescriptions, not least those of the New International Economic Order and the Brandt reports, assumes there is already a world society with a common set of ethical beliefs which
the technical economist can take for granted and use to make
judgements encompassing both the efficiency and equity components of economic welfare. But casual empiricism is enough to
show that there is no such world society; and nor is there a common view, shared by mankind, about the content of social justice.
Equally serious, even if we accept a utilitarian framework for measuring the interpersonal changes in welfare flowing from particular
economic changes, we cannot – as many economists seek to do –
identify equity and efficiency as the sole ends of *social* welfare. As
is evident from the writings of economists who have considered
the philosophical basis of welfare economics (Little and Sen, for
example), at best, only *economic* welfare can be identified with
these ends. Within the Western moral framework, other ends
such as 'liberty' are also valued and must be included in a judgement of the overall *ethical* desirability of a particular social order.
Thus, even if the calculus of utility can show that an egalitarian distribution of assets and a well-functioning market mechanism will
lead to the maximum 'social' welfare, we cannot *on this basis alone*
endorse a redistribution of assets or incomes. For, if the redistribution entails costs in terms of other social ends which are equally
valued, it would be foolish to disregard them and concentrate
solely on the strictly 'economic' ends.

---

1   Sen [189], Lal [105, 118].

There is, therefore, likely to be little agreement about either the content of 'distributive justice' or whether we should seek to achieve it through some form of coercive redistribution of incomes and assets when this would infringe other moral ends, such as 'liberty' which are equally valued. By contrast, most moral codes accept the view that, to the extent feasible, it is desirable to alleviate abject, absolute poverty or destitution. That alleviating poverty is not synonymous with reducing the inequality of income, as some seem still to believe,[2] can be seen by considering a country with the following two options. The first option leads to a rise in the incomes of all groups, including the poor, but to larger relative increases for the rich, and hence a worsening of the distribution of income. The second leads to no income growth for the poor but to a reduction in the income of the rich; thus the distribution of income improves but the extent of poverty remains unchanged. Those concerned with inequality would favour the second option, those with poverty the first.

Surplus labour, growth and labour incomes

The shades of Malthus and Marx have haunted development economics, particularly its preoccupation with equity and the alleviation of poverty. One of the major assertions of development economists in the 1950s, obsessed with so-called 'vicious circles' of poverty, was that the fruits of 'capitalist growth', with its reliance on the price mechanism, would not 'trickle down' or spread to the poor. Various *dirigiste* arguments were then advocated to bring the

---

2 For instance, Griffin and James [63], and my review in *Third World Quarterly*, June 1982.

poor into a growth process which would otherwise by-pass them. The most influential, as well as the most famous, of the models of development advanced in the 1950s to chart the likely course of outputs and incomes in an over-populated country or region was that of Sir Arthur Lewis.[3] It made an assumption of 'surplus labour' (below, p. 154) which, in a capitalist growth process, entailed that there would be no rise in the incomes of labour until the surplus had been absorbed.

The so-called 'Lewis dual economy' model assumed a backward sector, usually (but not necessarily) identified with subsistence agriculture, which suffered from population pressure in that the maximum amount of labour which could be productively used was being supplied by too many hands putting in too few hours individually. There was thus under-employment of labour on the land available, in the sense of a surplus of *labour time* relative to some *normal* number of working hours per worker per day.[4] These rural under-employed, it was argued, provided the nascent modern sector (usually identified with industry) with a completely elastic supply of labour at a wage just above the subsistence wage in agriculture. Given unchanged agricultural techniques, the pace of industrial development (industrial profits being largely invested) would thus determine the pace of economic growth. In such a growth process, fuelled by industrialisation, socially costless rural

3 Lewis [126].
4 Early refutations of the surplus labour theory are to be found in Haberler [65], Viner [210], Schultz [181]. It is difficult to see what use can be made of the numerous measures of surplus labour time which were subsequently derived. These measures, I submit, would be useful only for the commandant of a concentration camp or a slave driver! For a survey of studies which have attempted to estimate the extent of surplus labour time in numerous developing countries, Kao *et al.* [89].

VELOPMENT ECONOMICS'

EMPLOYMENT

put to productive industrial use. But during the
lus labour' phase of development, the wages of
not rise since, *ex hypothesi*, workers would be available in ited supply at the subsistence rural wage until they
ceased to be under-employed in agriculture. The aggregate increase in income generated by industrial growth would accrue
wholly to industrial capitalists in this early phase of development.

It was soon shown[5] that the assumptions required for even un-
deremployed rural labourers to be 'surplus' in Lewis's sense of
their being available to industry at a constant wage were very stringent, and implausible. It was necessary to assume that, with the
departure to the towns of their relatives, those rural workers who
remained would work harder for an unchanged wage. This implied that the preferences of rural workers between leisure and income are perverse, for workers will not usually work harder
without being offered a higher wage. Recent empirical research
into the shape of the supply curve of rural labour at different wages
has found that – at least for India, the country supposedly con-
taining vast pools of surplus labour – the curve is upward-sloping
(and not flat, as the surplus labour theory presupposes). Thus, increases in the demand for labour time, in both the industrial and
the rural sectors, can be satisfied only by paying higher wages.[6]

The fruits of growth, even in India, will therefore trickle down
in the sense either of raising labour incomes whenever the demand
for labour time increases by more than its supply or of preventing
the fall in real wages and thus labour incomes which would otherwise occur if the supply of labour time outstripped the increase in

5   Sen [187, 188].
6   Lal [106], Rosenzweig [178], Bardhan [15], Binswanger and Evenson [29],
     Bertrand and Squire [23].

demand for it. More direct evidence about mo
and industrial real wages of unskilled labour in d
tries for which data are available has shown that the st
nomic presumption that real wages will rise as the dem
labour grows, relative to its supply, is as valid for the Third W
as for the First![7]

'Unemployment' and poverty

The explosion of population in many developing countries, resulting from the reduction in death rates made possible by the spread
of modern medicine, has raised their labour supply and given rise
to fears of chronic mass unemployment. The so-called employment problem came to the forefront in the late 1960s on the assumption that the poor and unemployed were identical – as is
plausible in most developed economies. Empirical evidence
showed, however, that the unemployed in developing countries
were usually younger, more educated and more prosperous than
the employed.[8] This is not surprising since unemployment has to
be financed and, in the absence of unemployment insurance, only
the relatively wealthier can afford the luxury of being unemployed
in search of better jobs than are currently available. Moreover, unlike in industrial societies, much employment in most
pre-industrial and agrarian economies of the Third World is self-
employment. Thus, not surprisingly, the poor were found not
among the unemployed seeking jobs with high incomes and status, but among self-employed small traders, family workers, small

---

7   Squire [196] for a general survey of the evidence; Lal [119] for the evidence from
     India.
8   Squire [196].

ements in the rural
eveloping coun-
andard eco-
and for
rld

y could not be considered
long hours but for low re-
became subsumed in the

nployment and poverty was
writings on the 'state of the
s.[9] They had their origins in
s of poverty, destitution and
f the feudal system. Altruism
apart, it was ....r from vagrancy which lent ur-
gency to the need to find mea... of alleviating poverty, once the
link between poverty, crime and vice was perceived. Similar fears
underlay the concern in the Third World about their fast-growing
cities burgeoning with unemployed or under-employed poor im-
migrants from rural areas who could not be productively employed at reasonable incomes, given the additions to the capital
stock that were feasible. More seriously, even if capital formation
was rapid and the demand for unskilled labour could (at least in
principle) be raised, both unspecified institutional factors and the
use of inappropriate technologies would ensure that higher incomes would be garnered by the few, in the form of monopoly
profits or rents to skilled labour, with little 'trickledown' to the
poor. Some analysts went so far as to argue that the growth
process in Third World countries would lead to the immiseration
of the poor.[10] Rapid growth, it was increasingly claimed in the late
1960s and 1970s, could not be expected to alleviate poverty; and

---

9   Schumpeter [183], p. 220.
10 For instance, Adelman and Morris [2], ILO [83], Griffin [61].

special *dirigiste* measures were therefore recommended to modify technologies or increase the redistribution of assets or directly provide for the so-called 'basic needs' of the poor.'[11]

Those concerned with inequality devoted much effort to estimating empirically the so-called 'Kuznets curve', albeit on the basis of highly dubious distributional data from a host of developing countries.[12] The curve was used to illustrate a kind of iron law of distribution and development which said that, in the absence of redistributive policies, as per capita incomes increased the path of income distribution would follow the pattern of an inverted 'U', with a low degree of inequality at low levels of income rising to a peak at an income of about \$200–500 per head (in 1971 money values) and then declining. Anand and Kanbur[13] have, however, found that, even if the highly dubious data from which the Kuznets curve has been derived are accepted as sound, the curve which (statistically) represents the closest relationship between an index of inequality and per capita incomes is the converse of the Kuznets one – that is, it is U-shaped!

Nor have the gloomy inferences drawn from highly-aggregated data (pooled across countries) about the link between poverty and the growth rate of income stood up more successfully to detailed examination. Adelman and Morris claimed to have discovered, from cross-country comparisons of poverty and income growth, that 'development is accompanied by an absolute as well as a relative decline in the average income of the very poor'.[14] Apart from the fact that little can be usefully said by merely comparing at such

---

11   F. Stewart [199], Chenery *et al.* [40], ILO [82].

12   Ahluwalia [4].

13   S. Anand and R. Kanbur [6].

14   Adelman and Morris [2], p. 189.

aggregated levels the extent of poverty and growth rates across countries at a point in time, even the inferences drawn by Adelman and Morris from their own data were shown to be false.[15] Studies, still at a highly aggregated level, which charted the extent of poverty in fast- and slow-growing countries, found that growth certainly helped to reduce it – as its spectacular alleviation in the fast-growing East Asian economies testifies. And poverty did not necessarily increase in slow-growing or stagnant economics, as the examples of India and Sri Lanka show.[16]

Most of the studies which attempt to measure poverty accept the notion of an absolute level applicable to all the countries of the Third World. The poverty lines drawn by various international agencies have been based on nutritional considerations. However, it is doubtful whether a minimum nutritional standard for a country's population can be clearly defined, since individual food requirements vary enormously and no single calorific measure can be taken to define the minimum food requirements before malnutrition sets in.[17] As a result, not too much should be read into the numbers bandied about on the extent of absolute poverty – by, for instance, various international agencies and the Brandt Commission. They are probably most useful in identifying the countries and groups of countries where, even though no precise figures about absolute poverty are available, extreme poverty is most likely to exist. World Bank estimates[18] suggest that the world's poor are mainly in rural areas and that they are small farmers, landless labourers and various self-employed artisans, as well as

---

15   Cline [43], Lal [106], Ahluwalia [4].

16   For a survey of this evidence, Fields [57].

17   T. N. Srinivasan [197].

18   *World Development Report*, 1980, pp. 533–35.

small traders, low-earning urban self-employed (such as shoe-shine boys), and unskilled wage-earners not lucky enough to get a job in the relatively high-wage industrial sector. Their poverty is largely explained by the paucity of their assets and skills.

Rural development

Since Third World poverty is mainly rural, it is perhaps surprising that development economics was marked in its early days by little concern for rural development. The policy conclusions drawn from Lewis-type models of 'dual economies' (though, it should be emphasised, not by Lewis himself) were that agriculture would continue to stagnate and that industrialisation was the engine of growth. The protective systems erected to foster industry indirectly subsidised it at the expense of agriculture by raising the relative prices of manufactured inputs into agriculture. And the availability of surplus food-grains from the USA meant that, at least during the 1950s, countries like India could neglect their agricultural sectors without fear of a shortage of food. A shortage did, however, emerge as populations expanded rapidly and US food aid began to dry up. Moreover, the development of a new technology for producing hybrid wheat, and later rice, also led to a change in development policy in many countries.

The implicit assumption underlying the former neglect of agriculture – that peasants in the Third World were not responsive to prices and other incentives – was examined and shown to be wrong.[19] In the areas where it was feasible to use the new agricul-

---

19   Dharm Narain [164], Raj Krishna [95], Behrman [19], amongst numerous studies showing the price responsiveness of Third World farmers. Also, Schultz [182].

tural technology, namely, those with an assured water supply from irrigation where complementary inputs like fertilisers were available at prices reflecting their real cost to the economy and where the domestic prices of agricultural commodities were not kept too low in relation to their world prices, the farmers responded enthusiastically.[20] The Green Revolution had come about. It is still primarily a wheat revolution since the new rice technology requires much more control over water supplies than is usually possible in many LDCs. Because an assured water supply is required for ecological reasons, the Green Revolution has tended to accentuate inequalities between irrigated and dry farming areas. Nevertheless, where it has taken root it has transformed the standard of living of all strata of the population – as well as keeping food supplies in large consuming nations like India just ahead of the growth of population. Since the technology of the Green Revolution calls for a large increase in the demand for labour[21] – except in rural areas where (essentially because of the cheapening of the price of capital goods) large-scale mechanisation has accompanied its introduction – the real wages of agricultural labour and thus the incomes of the poor have been raised.

It is not surprising that, on the Left, the Green Revolution has been looked upon as a mixed blessing! Many Marxists who had based their hopes of a Third World political revolution on an increasingly impoverished peasantry sought to argue that the Green Revolution, far from alleviating rural poverty, was exacerbating it. The evidence for their counter-intuitive claim has been shown to be false. Despite their continued outpourings on the subject, it is

---

20   World Bank's *World Development Report, 1982* [214].
21   Johnston and Kilb y [88].

fair to say that the empirical evidence again supports the obvious economic argument that a large increase in the demand for rural labour relative to its supply will raise the earnings of all classes of the poor.[22]

This new, technologically-based agricultural revolution does, however, require substantial government support. For the agricultural research on which it is based has to be continuous and be tailored to the particular soil and climatic conditions of narrowly-defined ecological regions. Since this research produces new seeds which could easily be stolen if they were produced by private research, it clearly has external effects requiring it to be undertaken under government aegis.[23] Similarly, where an assured water supply can be provided at the lowest social cost through large-scale surface irrigation schemes such as dams and irrigation channels, it may be more efficient for government to assume the responsibility. Provision of irrigation water shares the characteristics of many public utilities and would require, at the least, some government regulation. Finally, there may be a role for government in disseminating information about the new technology by using extension workers to teach farmers the new agricultural techniques. There is thus a substantial role for governments in promoting rural development. It is, however, by no means usual for them to fulfil the role adequately or efficiently in the Third World despite the widespread adherence to *dirigisme* there.

---

22 For a survey of the evidence from a number of different countries, Vernon Ruttan [179]. For a detailed refutation of the various propositions about the effects of agricultural growth on the rural poor in South Asia, I. J. Singh [193]. Also Castillo [38] for the Philippines.

23 The classic statement of this need for rational *dirigisme* in agriculture is contained in Schultz [181].

Land reform

Many development economists, as well as laymen, have argued with some passion that another essential task of government is to ensure equitable rural development through land reform – either to break up larger farms into smaller ones or to consolidate the ownership of many small holdings. In countries such as South Korea, Taiwan and Japan, successful land reforms implemented under American compulsion promoted rapid and egalitarian rural development. The main argument for these reforms was that they could raise rural productivity, as well as improving the distribution of assets in the countryside. The efficiency gains claimed for land reforms were derived from empirical findings that the productivity per acre of land was higher on small than on large farms, particularly in South and South-East Asia. This result was supposed to stem from the higher levels of inputs which small farms using cheaper family labour were able to apply to the land, compared with larger farms which depended on hiring more expensive wage-labour. The scope and even desirability of such land reforms have, however, recently been disputed.[24]

Even in densely populated areas such as South Asia and parts of South-East Asia, where rural poverty is at its most acute, the scope for land redistribution is limited because the holdings are already very small. Breaking them up even more would provide little extra land for the landless; nor would it lead to any large gain in output. The latter conclusion is reinforced by recent research which shows that the earlier empirical finding that, in Asia, small farms based on family labour had higher levels of output than either larger farms based on hired labour or share-croppers no

---

24   Berry and Cline [22]; *World Development Report, 1982* [214], p. 84.

longer holds once adjustments are made for the quality of land.[25] Thus the gains in output from a land reform may be limited in Asia. Moreover, given the political difficulties in instituting such reforms, the continued debate about their feasibility and desirability may be discouraging landlords from investing in their land by heightening their feelings of insecurity.

The likely effects on productivity of land reform in the less densely settled areas of Africa and Latin America, where farm sizes are very much larger than in Asia but where land is also less scarce relative to population, remains a highly controversial issue. It would be fair to say, however, that, given the difficulties involved in implementing successful land reform in most countries, its benefits are unlikely to be as large in practice as its advocates claim. Moreover, land reform is neither a necessary nor a sufficient condition for equitable rural development as long as the markets for rural labour and agricultural commodities are not too imperfect.[26]

Despite systems of tenure which are less than ideal, there is little evidence that agricultural growth within the existing agrarian structures of most developing countries will damage the interests of the poor. Rather, the likelihood is that efficient rural development in most Third World countries will strongly alleviate poverty by raising the incomes of smallholders directly and those of landless labourers through the increase in demand for their labour which the new technology brings. The problem lies in the sins of both omission and commission of public policy. It

---

25   *Ibid.*
26   For a survey of the evidence on the functioning of rural labour markets, Binswanger and Rosenzweig [30].

is the inadequate provision of an agricultural infrastructure, together with the distortion of agricultural incentives common in many developing countries but particularly acute in parts of sub-Saharan Africa, which explains the relatively disappointing performance in agriculture, and thus in alleviating rural poverty.[27] Only policy differences can explain the variations in agricultural productivity among countries with similar resources and agrarian structures.[28] Historically, as well as in the post-war period, an agricultural revolution has always either preceded or accompanied industrial development. The fastest-growing countries have experienced high rates of expansion of both agriculture and industry. The laggards, such as Ghana and Tanzania,[29] have been those which either neglected their agriculture in attempting to force industrialisation or sought to impose some form of collectivisation in line with the prescriptions of many influential development economists in the 1950s and 1960s.

It remains, however, true that, in most densely-populated countries where the labour force can be expected to continue to expand for the next 50 years,[30] an increasing share of output and employment will have to be found in industry and services during the course of development. Paradoxically, the failure of most South

---

27 World Bank [213].

28 Thus the World Bank's *World Development Report, 1982* [214] states: 'Despite the similar resources and history of the countries, agricultural productivity has increased twice as fast in Cameroon and Liberia in recent years as it has in neighbouring Guinea and Ghana – and four times as fast in Tunisia and Colombia as in Morocco and Peru' (p. 45).

29 The explicit link between Nkrumah's acceptance of the advice of the then fashionable development economists and the subsequent development disaster which befell Ghana is clearly documented and dissected in Killick [92]. The Tanzanian development disaster is analysed by Coulson [48].

30 Squire [196].

Asian countries, in particular India, significantly to alleviate rural poverty has been due to their dismal industrial performance rather than to any marked reverses in rural development.[31] Their industrial failure, as was argued in Chapter 4, is due not to a lack of capital, entrepreneurship or skilled labour, but to misguided government intervention. Many of the world's poor are concentrated in the Indian sub-continent and alleviating their poverty calls for *efficient* industrial development, as well as continuing rural development. That will be possible only if the governments concerned eschew their almost blind attachment to the *Dirigiste Dogma*, which has done so little for either the quality or rate of growth of income per head in these countries.

Appropriate goods and technologies

Many seemingly new-fangled arguments in favour of even more *dirigisme* are, however, still being advocated. One flows from the correct observation that much industrial development, particularly in South Asia, has been based on capital-intensive technologies unsuited to countries endowed with abundant labour. But instead of emphasising that the inappropriate technology has been chosen because of the biased incentives created by protection – that is, the implicit cheapening of capital goods relative to the costs of labour through public policy – the problem is specified as one of a limited range of choice amongst available techniques to provide suitable labour-intensive technologies for development.[32] Various schemes for the development or invention of labour-

---

31   Lal [119].
32   Stewart [198].

intensive or appropriate technology through government-supported research are then advocated.[33] They are misguided for two reasons.

First, even if – as such arguments implicitly assume – a product can be made only with fixed coefficients relating inputs to outputs so that it is impossible to substitute labour for capital, different products will nevertheless have different (albeit fixed) capital-labour ratios. By making more labour-intensive *products*, a country faced with fixed and probably inappropriate technologies for each one can, if it chooses, produce a more labour-intensive bundle of products. Indeed, if the relative domestic price of capital to labour was not distorted by public policy as often as it is, domestic producers would choose both the most labour-intensive of available techniques and, in the aggregate, the most labour-intensive bundle of products. It is the desire for autarky, as well as the ideological predilection for heavy industry, which has led to the increasing capital intensity of Indian industry, for instance – and not any lack of technical substitutability, in the aggregate, between capital and labour in that country's industrial output.

Secondly, the *development* of new appropriate technologies is likely to demand skilled labour, such as engineers. The human capital embodied in them must be counted as part of the fixed capital cost of the resulting techniques. It is by no means clear that the appropriate technologies thus developed will be any less capital-intensive than the existing inappropriate ones they are invented to replace.

---

33 A more detailed discussion of the technical feasibility and economic desirability of appropriate techniques in different 'sectors' is in Lal [109], Appendix 1.

'Basic needs'

Another new-fangled argument for *dirigisme* is entailed in what has come to be labelled the 'basic needs' (BN) approach. Influenced by the continuing absolute poverty of millions in the Third World, many observers have despaired of being able to deal with it through what the ILO calls 'conventional high-growth' policies.[34] Instead, they would seek to meet the basic needs of the people by 'the production and delivery to the intended groups of the BN basket through "supply-management" and a "delivery system"'. The 'BN basket' consists of:

> First, ... various items of private consumption: food, shelter, clothing. Secondly, various public services such as drinking water, sanitation, public transport, health and educational facilities.

Thus a number of components of BN are publicly-provided services (though not necessarily public goods). The aim of the BN approach is to expand the supply of these basic services as well as to convert the bulk of private consumption into publicly-provided goods and services. The 'strategy' is fundamentally paternalistic, entailing a vast increase in state control and bureaucratic discretion.

The following kind of contrast is a persistent theme in the writings on BN.[35] First, even with efficient growth, poverty has not been alleviated to the extent possible because of various market imperfections. Secondly, a perfectly-functioning bureaucratic system of allocation can achieve the optimal degree of growth to alleviate poverty. The fallacy in this is obvious, as the last chapter sought to show.

---

34   ILO [82], p. 16.
35   The best of these is Streeten and Burki [205]. For critiques, Srinivasan [197], Lal [114].

THE POVERTY OF 'DEVELOPMENT ECONOMICS'

Yet various *dirigiste* régimes, such as Mrs Bandaranaike's Sri Lanka and Nyerere's Tanzania, which are cited as having achieved improvements in various indicators of the quality of life (such as longevity and literacy) even with little growth, are held up as the examples to be emulated.[36] On these indices of welfare improvement, the post-war period has been one of the most beneficial for all strata of Third World populations, compared with both their own historical experience and that of today's developed countries. It is argued, however, that the differences in growth performance among developing countries are not necessarily related to changes in these social indicators. Hence, income growth is not necessarily associated with the alleviation of poverty.

Amartya Sen has classified countries according to their respective performance in longevity and literacy.[37] He concludes that, for longevity, the communist countries have performed best. But the best performers in terms of *both* indicators are Taiwan, South Korea, Hong Kong, and Singapore. However, low-income countries like Sri Lanka (longevity) and Tanzania (literacy) are also relative success stories. Sen proceeds to argue that there are two ways of removing poverty:

> Ultimately, poverty removal must come to grips with the
> issue of entitlement guarantees. The two strategies differ in
> the means of achieving this guarantee. While one relies on
> the successfully fostered growth and the dynamism of the
> encouraged labour market, the other gives the government a
> more *direct* role as the provider of provisions.[38]

---

36   Isenman [85], Sen [191].
37   Sen [191].
38   *Ibid.*, p. 309.

This approach, however, glosses over the differences in the *nature of the guarantee* provided by each of these supposed ways of removing poverty. Not all guarantees are equally iron-clad! Despite stagnant economies, countries such as Sri Lanka and Tanzania have hitherto managed to operate social welfare programmes to meet so-called basic needs. The security of such politically-determined entitlements of the poor is, however, coming increasingly into question as the inexorable increase in their cost confronts a fixed economic pie from which to finance them.

By contrast, the poverty which, in the East Asian countries, has been alleviated through rising incomes cannot be so easily reversed by political fiat, since entitlements have been earned and are underwritten by the wealth created in the growth process. Moreover, there is good reason to believe that, by promoting efficiency, Sri Lanka and Tanzania could have achieved both growth and the alleviation of poverty – as Korea and Taiwan have done.[39]

Growth, or its quality, has been inadequate in many developing countries partly because their policies have been based on simplistic and one-dimensional notions of the dominant constraint, or bottleneck, on development. Many of the same people who are now wringing their hands at the insufficient alleviation of poverty by past growth were the proponents of various mechanistic models based on developmental gaps – such as skills, savings, and foreign exchange – which their particular 'strategy' was proposed to fill.[40]

---

39 It should be noted that more recent work questions the claims made in the past by acolytes of Maoism about the extent of *dirigiste* China's success in alleviating poverty or reducing inequality. (Eberstadt [56] and the recent World Bank report on China.)

40 Thus, Haq [68] and his recantation in Haq [69].

This intellectual framework has not changed. The new gap is between the different goods and services actually consumed by the Third World's poor and those deemed by technocrats to be necessary to meet basic needs. Filling that gap is considered to be a matter of social engineering, which the bureaucracies of the Third World can readily perform. Further support is thereby lent to their *dirigiste* impulses which, in attempting to supplant the price mechanism, have done so much indirect damage to the prospects of the Third World's poor. By not emphasising enough the inherent limitations of an imperfect bureaucracy at the same time as they castigate imperfect markets, those seeking to supplant the price mechanism in the provision of basic needs may yet again divert attention from the most important lesson of the varied development performance of the Third World in the last three decades, namely, that efficient growth which raises the demand for unskilled labour by 'getting the prices right' is probably the single most important means of alleviating poverty.

6 SOME GENERAL CONCLUSIONS

Underlying much of development economics is the quest for a new 'unorthodox' economics, of special application to the Third World, which surfaced in the early 1960s with a debate initiated by an influential article by the late Dudley Seers.[1] Those who sought a new economics claimed that the orthodox neo-classical model was (*a*) unrealistic because of its behavioural, technological and institutional assumptions, and (*b*) irrelevant because it was concerned primarily with the efficient allocation of given resources and hence could deal with neither so-called dynamic aspects of growth nor with various ethical aspects of the alleviation of poverty or the distribution of income. Yet, as Myint noted, most of the unorthodox economics then put on offer consisted of little more than

> selecting the 'queer cases' in the Western models of analysis
> and in taking it for granted that these exceptions to the
> standard case must automatically apply to the
> under-developed countries because they are so different
> from the advanced countries in their social attitudes and
> institutional setting.[2]

This paper has charted the various twists and turns that the unorthodox theories have subsequently taken. Mostly, they

---

1   Seers [186].
2   Myint [161], p. 70.

have sought to justify massive government intervention through forms of direct control usually intended to supplant the price mechanism. The empirical assumptions on which this *dirigisme* was based have been belied by the experience of numerous countries in the post-war period. The most serious current distortions in many developing economies are not those flowing from the inevitable imperfections of a market economy but the policy-induced, and thus far from inevitable, distortions created by irrational *dirigisme*. This concluding chapter sums up the reasons why the assumptions underlying the *dirigisme* promoted by development economics, however plausible they may have seemed in the 1950s or early 1960s, are no longer persuasive.

At its bluntest, behind at least part of the *dirigiste* case is a paternalistic attitude born of a distrust of, if not contempt for, the ordinary, poor, uneducated masses of the Third World. This attitude is not confined entirely, nor even primarily, to Western outsiders; it is shared by many in the ruling élites of the Third World. As a leading development economist has observed about Gunnar Myrdal, one of the Western economists to have fuelled the *Dirigiste Dogma*:

> As a proud, somewhat un-Swedish Swede ... he [Myrdal] finds it easier to identify with liberal Americans than with the English or French, and easier with Englishmen than with the Indian masses. It is partly for this reason that *An American Dilemma* is an optimistic book, and *Asian Drama* a pessimistic one. He once said how kindred American aspirations and ideals, and the 'American creed', were to his own beliefs, and how he could identify with these ideals when writing the book on the black problem; and how, in contrast, when he visited an Indian textile factory, the half-naked brown bodies struck him as utterly alien.[3]

It is easy to suppose that these half-starved, wretched and ignorant masses could not possibly conform, either as producers or consumers, to the behavioural assumption of orthodox neo-classical economics that 'people would act *economically;* when the opportunity of an advantage was presented to them they would take it'.[4] This has been termed the 'Economic Principle' by Hicks,[5] and denying it is the hallmark of much of development economics – together with the assertion that some ethereal and verbally sanitised entity (such as 'government', 'planners', or 'policy-makers') which is both knowledgeable and compassionate can overcome the defects of these stupid or ignorant producers and consumers and compel them to raise their living standards through various *dirigiste* means. As Myint has noted, the seemingly scientific language in which are couched these judgements questioning the validity of Western behavioural assumptions in other cultures is illusory:

> If one were to tell the politicians of the underdeveloped
> countries that their people are lazy, stupid, lacking in
> initiative and adaptability, one would be branded as an
> enemy; but if one were to rephrase these prejudices in
> another way and say that the people lack entrepreneurial
> capacity, one would be welcomed for giving 'scientific'
> support for economic planning.[6]

There is by now a vast body of empirical evidence from different cultures and climates which shows that uneducated peasants

---

3   Streeten [204], p. 425.
4   Hicks [77], p. 43.
5   *Ibid.*
6   Myint [161], p. 71.

act economically as producers and consumers.[7] They respond to changes in relative prices much as neo-classical economic theory predicts. The 'Economic Principle' is not unrealistic in the Third World.

Nor has experience proved the conventional technological assumptions of neo-classical theory (about the possibilities of substituting different inputs in production) to be unrealistic. The degree to which inputs of different factors and commodities can be substituted in the production of the national product is not much different in developed or developing countries.[8] Furthermore, it cannot be assumed that Third World labourers (and consumers) have such peculiar preferences that, when they become richer, by however small an amount and from however lowly a base, they will not also seek to increase their 'leisure'; putting it the other way round, for them as for workers in the developed world the cost of 'sweat' rises the harder and longer they have to work. No less than their Western counterparts, they are unlikely to be in 'surplus' in any meaningful economic sense.

Nor are the so-called institutional features of the Third World, such as their strange social and agrarian structures or their usurious informal credit systems, necessarily a handicap to growth.[9] Far from asserting that these institutions inhibit efficiency, conventional neo-classical theory is now seeking to show the precise

---

7 For references to numerous empirical studies, Nugent and Yotopoulos [166].

8 Morawetz [158]; Behrman [21].

9 Myrdal [163] emphasises the deleterious effects of these institutional factors on economic development in South Asia. Also, Madan [146] for an anthropological critique of Myrdal, and Lal [119] for an economic explanation of the origins and economic functions of caste.

sense in which they may promote it and is discovering that they are not as irrational and uneconomic as so many *dirigistes* claim. They are likely to represent an efficient, second-best adaptation to the risks and uncertainties inevitable in the relevant economic environment. In the absence of other means of eliminating or alleviating the risks, the destruction of these traditional institutions could actually do more harm than good.[10]

Imperfect markets superior to imperfect planning

Nor has experience proved the irrelevance of neo-classical allocation theory; quite the contrary. The centralised planning which *dirigistes* have sought to promote has the same intellectual basis as the efficient allocation of resources through the market mechanism extolled by neo-classical economics. As Myint has noted: 'Both accept the optimum allocation of resources as their theoretical norm and their disagreements are about the *practical* means of fulfilling this norm'.[11] This paper has given reasons, rooted both in the experience of developing countries and in theory, why, of the only feasible alternatives – a necessarily imperfect planning mechanism and a necessarily imperfect market mechanism – the latter is likely to perform better in practice. Finally, it is neo-classical economics which has provided the justification for *rational dirigisme*, by showing that there are methods of 'planning' through the price mechanism which may be both feasible and desirable.[12]

---

10 Braverman and Stiglitz [35], Bardhan [16], Braverman and Srinivasan [34] on the agrarian structure; Lal [113] for a survey of the literature on industrial wage structures; and Binswanger and Rosenzweig [30] on rural wage structures.

11 Myint [161], p. 73.

12 Lal [116] for an application to India, and Scott, MacArthur, Newberry [185] for Kenya.

It is true, however, that economic theory is unable to offer a rigorous account of the *process* of development, the so-called dynamic aspects which much concern some *dirigistes*. But neither have the latter succeeded in supplying an alternative theoretical framework for studying and influencing the dynamic processes. Their arguments for *dirigisme* based on so-called 'dynamic aspects' usually turn out to be either incoherent or merely handwaving.[13] More importantly, the belief that neo-classical economics is particularly unsuitable for analysing dynamic processes in developing (as contrasted with developed) countries is unlikely to be valid. The fundamental method of neo-classical economics is to compare alternative equilibrium states of the economy. But, like perfect competition, the equilibria are only notional – yet not for that reason to be despised. There has been much discussion of the notion of equilibrium in economic analysis, and many have concluded that it is irrelevant for understanding the workings of actual economies.

This paper cannot enter into these more theoretical debates. But, paradoxically, with its neglect of the adjustment process between two equilibria (at least in its most readily usable 'comparative statics' form) and its emphasis on the flexibility of the prices of both commodities and factors of production, neo-classical eco-

---

13 Thus, for instance, Hirschman has emphasised two seemingly unorthodox dynamic effects. The first are called backward and forward linkages of investments; the second is the so-called 'hiding hand' which turns apparently economically-disastrous projects into successes! These backward and forward linkages are, however, simply other names for the ubiquitous interdependence of production found in any moderately complex economy. It is doubtful, however, that the existence of these 'linkages' provides any special reasons for *dirigisme* (Little and Mirrlees [142]). The hiding hand' is equally unconvincing, and resorting to it would exclude the possibility of discriminating *ex ante* between good and bad projects, which is clearly absurd!

nomics is likely to be more applicable to developing than to developed countries. For, unlike in richer countries, economic agents in poor ones will have few 'reserves' to fall back upon and will thus have to adjust speedily to a change in their economic environment by swiftly altering the terms on which they are willing to exchange economic commodities. Though this may not always be desirable, it does mean that the simple stories derived from the comparative statistics method are not irrelevant. It is in the developed countries that economic agents, endowed with fairly large reserves in the form either of past savings or of entitlements provided by the welfare state, can postpone the required price adjustments in a changing economic environment. The so-called fixed-price markets for goods and factors in developed countries which allegedly call for a revision of neo-classical theory are thus unlikely to be widespread in most developing countries.

Moreover, there now exists a quite large number of what may be termed analytical economic histories (the only type of truly dynamic analysis available), of which the various studies of trade and industrialisation are most notable in allowing us to form judgements about the policies likely to foster development.[14] Yet there are people who will not find this sufficient in their search for the Holy Grail of the 'necessary and sufficient conditions for development'.[15] It should be obvious that economics cannot hope to provide such conditions. What the experience of developing countries

---

14   The OECD, World Bank and NBER studies cited earlier. Also, ILO [81] on the Philippines; Galenson (ed.) [59] on Taiwan; and a series of studies edited by Ed. Mason for the Harvard Institute of Development on Korea. Collier and Lal [44] on Kenya, and Lal [119] on India, seek to provide explicit analytical economic histories of these countries, primarily on the evolution of labour incomes and labour institutions.

15   This seems to be what Stewart and Streeten [201] are seeking.

does show is that, other things equal, the most important advice that economists can currently offer is that of Stewart and Streeten's so-called Price Mechanist: 'Get the prices right'.[16]

Unlamented demise of 'development economics'

It is in the political and administrative aspects of *dirigisme* that powerful practical arguments can be advanced against the *Dirigiste Dogma*. The political and administrative assumptions underlying the feasibility of various forms of *dirigisme* derive from those of modern welfare states in the West. These, in turn, reflect the values of the 18th-century Enlightenment. It has taken nearly two centuries of political evolution for those values to be internalised and reflected (however imperfectly) in the political and administrative institutions of Western societies. In the Third World, an acceptance of the same values is at best confined to a small class of Westernised intellectuals. Despite their trappings of modernity, many developing countries are closer in their official workings to the rapacious and inefficient nation-states of 17th- or 18th-century Europe, governed as much for the personal aggrandisement of their rulers as for the welfare of the ruled. It is instructive to recall that Keynes, who so many *dirigistes* invoke as a founding father of their faith, noted in *The End of Laissez-Faire:*

> But above all, the ineptitude of public administrators strongly prejudiced the practical man in favour of *laissez-faire* – a sentiment which has by no means disappeared. Almost everything which the State did in the 18th century in excess of its minimum functions was, or seemed, injurious or unsuccessful.[17]

16   Stewart and Streeten [201].

It is in this context that anyone familiar with the actual administration and implementation of policies in very many Third World countries, and not blinkered by the *Dirigiste Dogma*, should find that oft-neglected work, *The Wealth of Nations*, both so relevant and so modern. For in most of our modern-day equivalents of the inefficient 18th-century state, not even the minimum governmental functions required for economic progress are always fulfilled. Yet the *dirigistes* have been urging a myriad new tasks on Third World governments which go well beyond what Keynes considered to be a sensible agenda for *mid-20th-century* Western politics:

> The most important *Agenda* of the State relate not to those activities which private individuals are already fulfilling, but to those functions which fall outside the sphere of the individual, to those decisions which are made by no one if the State does not make them. The important thing for governments is not to do things which individuals are doing already, and to do them a little better or a little worse; but to do those things which at present are not done at all.[18]

This is a far cry from that 'enlightened discrimination' towards foreign trade, transnational companies, technology, and the meeting of basic needs currently being touted as desirable for developing countries.[19] In these deeply ideological times, it may be vain to

---

17   Keynes [91], p. 12.

18   Ibid., pp. 46–7.

19   Streeten [203]. As Little [137] has rightly remarked: 'Of course, such a position always puts the critic at some disadvantage, because he seldom wants to advocate *laissez-faire*, and the policies described will usually contain some elements that he would himself advocate – for example, export taxes or hard case-by-case bargaining in the case of mineral exploitation. Nevertheless, the picture of "enlightened discrimination" drawn by Streeten seems to me to come too close to

hope to steer a middle course between *laissez-faire* and the *Dirigiste Dogma*. In the light of the foregoing, however, and the repeated trouncing of development economics, the author, for one, cannot join Hirschman in lamenting its fall. The major conclusion of this paper is that the demise of development economics is likely to be conducive to the health of both the economics and the economies of developing countries.

Indian policy over the past twenty years, and too close to maximum surveillance and control for it to be likely to do anything but retard growth without any off-setting benefit. There is a mass of evidence, in works already cited and elsewhere, that discrimination is seldom very enlightened.'

APPENDIX

A GUIDE TO 'SECOND-BEST' WELFARE THEORY

In describing and (where empirically possible) measuring the deviation of an economy from the perfectly-competitive norm, it has been found useful to define the deviations as 'distortions' of the relative prices (and thence quantities) of commodities in an actual economy compared with those which would prevail in the hypothetically perfectly-competitive one. In the latter, market prices of goods and factors of production would equate and would equal the marginal social cost (MSC) of producing (equal to the producer's price) and the marginal social value (MSV) of using (equal to the consumer price) the relevant goods or factors. Decentralised decisions about investment, production and consumption would be socially as well as privately optimal. A market imperfection drives a wedge, as it were, between the MSC and MSV of a commodity and causes them to diverge from the market price. This wedge is the 'distortion' referred to. In principle, it can be removed by lump-sum taxes and subsidies, so that the tax/subsidy-inclusive market price *does* equate the MSC and MSV of the relevant good. If, however, government cannot use lump-sum taxes and subsidies for any reason, the use of another fiscal device (such as direct or indirect taxation) or administrative controls will, whilst closing the gap between MSC and MSV for the initial commodity, open up other wedges between MSCs and MSVs elsewhere in the economy. The welfare *losses* from the opening up of these new wedges (called 'by-product distortion' costs) which are an inevitable consequence of non-lump-sum fiscal devices must be balanced against the *gains* from deploying them to offset the primary distortion between MSC and MSV.

Let us consider decreasing-cost industries. In a perfectly competitive economy the price consumers pay measures the MSV of the good and equals the marginal cost of production, which is its MSC. For producers to be willing to sell this good at a price which equals its *marginal* cost of production, they must at least be able to cover the total cost of production. If there are decreasing costs in the industry, the *average* cost of producing a given output is *higher* than the *marginal* cost, so that producers would make a loss if they priced the good at its marginal cost. They will, therefore, not be willing to equate price with the marginal cost of production unless (at the least) they are provided with a subsidy equal to the difference between the average and marginal costs. But if government gives them a subsidy (to ensure the perfectly competitive outcome), it will have to raise taxes to finance it. Let us suppose it levies an indirect tax on some other commodity to finance the subsidy. The indirect tax will raise the final price of that commodity. And so the initial equality, *ex hypothesi*, between *its* MSC and MSV will be disturbed since the consumer price (which measures the MSV) will now be higher than the unchanged marginal cost (which measures the MSC) of the taxed good. By curing the divergence between the MSC and MSV of the decreasing-cost industry through a subsidy, government has had to introduce a new divergence between the MSC and MSV of another good.

The *net* effect of an increase in welfare from closing the initial divergence between MSC and MSV and a decrease in welfare from opening the new 'by-product' divergence cannot be known *a priori*. If there is a net loss, *it may be 'second-best' (which is all that is feasible) to do nothing.*

REFERENCES FOR 1983 TEXT

[1]   S. N. Acharya: 'Perspectives and Problems of
        Development in Low Income Sub-Saharan Africa', in S. N.
        Acharya and Bruce Johnston, *Two Studies of Development in
        Sub-Saharan Africa*, World Bank Staff Working Paper No.
        300, Washington DC, October 1978.

[2]   I. Adelman and C. T. Morris: *Economic Growth and Social
        Equity in Developing Countries*, Stanford, 1973.

[3]   A. N. Agarwala and S. P. Singh (eds.): *The Economics of
        Underdevelopment*, Oxford University Press, London, 1958.

[4]   M. Ahluwalia: 'Inequality, Poverty and Development',
        Journal of Development Economics, 1976.

[5]   S. Amin: *Unequal Development*, Harvester Press, Sussex.

[6]   S. Anand and R. Kanbur (forthcoming).

[7]   K. J. Arrow: 'Political and Economic Evaluation of Social
        Effects and Externalities', in J. Margolis (ed.), *The Analysis
        of Public Output*, NBER, Columbia, New York, 1970.

[8]   E. L. Bacha and C. F. Diaz-Alejandro: *International
        Financial Intermediation: A Long and Tropical View*,
        Princeton University Essays in International Finance, No.
        147, Princeton, 1982.

[9]   A. K. Bagchi: *Private Investment in India – 1900–1939*,
        Cambridge, 1972.

[10]   A. K. Bagchi: 'De-Industrialisation in India in the 19th
       Century: Some Theoretical Implications', *Journal of
       Development Studies*, Vol. 12, No. 2, 1976.

[11]   B. Balassa: *The Structure of Protection in Developing
       Countries*, Johns Hopkins University Press, Baltimore, 1971.

[12]   B. Balassa: 'Prospects for Trade in Manufactured Goods
       Between Industrial and Developing Countries, 1978–1990',
       Journal of Policy Modelling, Vol. 2, No. 3, 1980; reprinted in
       World Bank Reprint Series No. 156.

[13]   B. Balassa: *Development Strategies in Semi-Industrial
       Economies*, Johns Hopkins, 1982.

[14]   T. Balogh: *Unequal Partners*, 2 vols., Blackwells, Oxford,
       1963.

[15]   P. K. Bardhan: 'Labour Supply Functions in a Poor
       Agrarian Economy', *American Economic Review*, March 1979.

[16]   P. K. Bardhan: 'Interlocking Factor Markets and Agrarian
       Development: A Review of Issues', *Oxford Economic Papers*,
       March 1980.

[17]   P. T. Bauer: 'Foreign Aid: An Instrument for Progress?', in
       B. Ward and P. T. Bauer, *Two Views on Aid to Developing
       Countries*, Occasional Paper No. 9, Institute of Economic
       Affairs, London, 1966.

[18]   P. T. Bauer and B. S. Yamey: *The Economics of
       Underdeveloped Countries*, Cambridge, 1957.

[19]   J. R. Behrman: *Supply Response in Underdeveloped
       Agriculture*, North Holland, Amsterdam, 1968.

[20]   J. R. Behrman: *International Commodity Agreements*: an
       evaluation of the UNCTAD integrated commodity
       programme, Monograph No. 9, Overseas Development
       Council, Washington DC, 1977.

[21]   J. R. Behrman: 'Review Article on Hollis Chenery:
         Structural Change in Development Policy', *Journal of
         Development Economics*, June 1982.
[22]   R. A. Berry and W. R. Cline: *Agrarian Structure and
         Productivity in Developing Countries*, Johns Hopkins
         University Press, 1978.
[23]   T. J. Bertrand and L. Squire: 'The Relevance of the Dual
         Economy Model: A Case Study of Thailand', *Oxford
         Economic Papers*, November 1980.
[24]   J. N. Bhagwati: *Anatomy and Consequences of Trade Control
         Régimes*, National Bureau of Economic Research, New
         York, 1979.
[25]   J. N. Bhagwati and P. Desai: *India – Planning for
         Industrialisation*, Oxford, 1970.
[26]   J. N. Bhagwati and V. K. Ramaswami: 'Domestic
         Distortions and the Theory of Optimum Subsidy', *Journal
         of Political Economy*, February 1963.
[27]   J. N. Bhagwati and T. N. Srinivasan: *Foreign Trade Régimes
         and Economic Development – India*, NBER, Columbia
         University Press, 1975.
[28]   D. Bhattacharya: *A Concise History of the Indian Economy,
         1750–1950*, 2nd Edition, Prentice-Hall of India, New Delhi,
         1979.
[29]   H. P. Binswanger and R. E. Evenson: 'Estimating Labour
         Demand Functions for Indian Agriculture', mimeo, ADC/
         ICRISAT Conference, Hyderabad, 1980, to be published in
         the conference proceedings by Yale University Press.
[30]   H. Binswanger and M. Rosenzweig: 'Contractual
         Arrangements, Employment and Wages in Rural Labour
         Markets – A Critical Review', mimeo, Studies in

Employment and Rural Development No. 67, World Bank, Washington DC, June 1981, to be published as an introduction to a book of ADC/ICKISAT papers by Yale University Press.

[31] R. Blackhurst, N. Marian, J. Tumlir: *Trade Liberalisation, Protectionism and Interdependence*, GATT Studies in International Trade No. 5, GATT, Geneva, November 1977.

[32] Brandt Report: *North-South – A Programme for Survival*, The Report of the Independent Commission on International Development Issues under the Chairmanship of Willy Brandt, Pan Books, London, 1980.

[33] Brandt Commission: *Common Crisis – North-South: Co-operation for World Recovery*, Pan Books, London, 1983.

[34] A. Braverman and T. N. Srinivasan: 'Credit and Share Cropping in Agrarian Societies', *Journal of Development Economics*, 1982.

[35] A. Braverman and J. Stiglitz: 'Sharecropping and the Interlinking of Agrarian Markets', *American Economic Review*, September 1982.

[36] M. Bronfrenbrenner: 'A Simplified Mahalanobis Development Model', *Economic Development and Cultural Change*, University of Chicago, Vol. X, 1960.

[37] A. K. Cairncross: *Factors in Economic Development*, Macmillan, 1962.

[38] G. Castillo: *All in a Grain of Rice – A Review of Philippines Studies on the Social and Economic Implications of the New Rice Technology*, S.E. Asian Regional Centre for Graduate Study and Research in Agriculture, Los Banos, Philippines, 1975.

[39] H. Chenery: 'The Interdependence of Investment Decisions', in A. Abramowitz (ed.), *The Allocation of Economic Resources*, Stanford, 1959.

[40] H. Chenery et al.: *Redistribution with Growth*, Oxford, 1974.

[41] H. Chenery et al.: *Structural Change and Development Policy*, Oxford, 1979.

[42] H. Chenery and A. M. Strout: 'Foreign Assistance and Economic Development', *American Economic Review*, September 1966.

[43] W. R. Cline: 'Distribution and Development – A Survey of the Literature', *Journal of Development Economics*, 1975.

[44] P. Collier and D. Lal: *Poverty and Growth in Kenya*, World Bank Staff Working Paper No. 389, 1980.

[45] P. Collier and D. Lal: 'Coercion, Compassion and Competition – Wage and Employment Trends and Structure in Kenya 1800–1980', mimeo, Studies in Employment and Rural Development, No. 64, World Bank, 1981.

[46] W. M. Corden: *Trade Policy and Economic Welfare*, Oxford, 1974.

[47] W. M. Corden: *The NIEO Proposals: A Cool Look*, Thames Essay No. 21, Trade Policy Research Centre, London, 1979.

[48] A Coulson: *Tanzania – A Political Economy*, Oxford, 1982.

[49] P. Dasgupta, S. Marglin and A. K. Sen: *Guidelines for Project Evaluation*, UNIDO, New York, 1972.

[50] P. Deane: *The Evolution of Economic Ideas*, Cambridge, 1978.

[51] C. Diaz-Alejandro: 'Delinking North and South: Unshackled or Unhinged?', in A. Fishlow et al., *Rich and Poor Nations in the World Economy*, McGraw Hill, New York, 1978.

[52]   J. B. Donges: 'A Comparative Survey of Industrialisation
        Policies in 15 Semi-industrial Countries',
        Weltwirtschaftliches Archiv, Band 112, Heft 4, 1976.

[53]   R. C. Dutt: *The Economic History of India*, Vols. I and II,
        Routledge, London, 1901.

[54]   J. Eaton and M. Gersovitz: *Poor Country Borrowing in
        Private Financial Markets and the Repudiation Issue*,
        Princeton Studies in International Finance No. 47,
        Princeton, June 1981.

[55]   A. Emmanuel: *Unequal Exchange*, Monthly Review Press,
        New York, 1972.

[56]   N. Eberstadt: 'Has China Failed?', *New York Review of
        Books*, Vol. XXVI, Nos. 5, 6, and 7, April–May 1978.

[57]   G. S. Fields: *Poverty, Inequality and Development*,
        Cambridge, 1980.

[58]   R. Findlay: 'The Fundamental Determinants of the Terms
        of Trade', in Grassman and Lundberg (eds.) [60].

[59]   W. Galenson (ed.): *Economic Growth and Structural Change
        in Taiwan*, Cornell, 1979.

[60]   S. Grassman and E. Lundberg (eds.): *The World Economic
        Order: Past and Prospects*, Macmillan, 1981.

[61]   K. Griffin: *The Political Economy of Agrarian Change*,
        Macmillan, 1974.

[62]   K. Griffin and J. Enos: 'Foreign Assistance: Objectives and
        Consequences', *Economic Development and Cultural
        Change*, April 1970.

[63]   K. Griffin and J. James: *The Transition to Egalitarian
        Development*, Macmillan, 1981.

[64]   G. Haberler: 'Some Problems in the Pure Theory of
        International Trade', *Economic Journal*, 1950.

[65] G. Haberler: 'Critical Observations on Some Current Notions in the Theory of Economic Development', *L'Industria*, No. 2, 1957, reprinted in G. Meier (ed.) [153].

[66] G. Haberler: A *Survey of International Trade Theory*, Princeton Special Papers in International Economics, 1961.

[67] F. H. Hahn: 'On Optimum Taxation', *Journal of Economic Theory*, February 1973.

[68] M. Haq: *The Strategy of Economic Development*, Oxford, 1963.

[69] M. Haq: *The Poverty Curtain*, Columbia, 1976.

[70] A. C. Harberger: *Project Evaluation – Selected Essays*, Chicago, 1972.

[71] F. A. Hayek (ed.): *Collectivist Economic Planning*, Routledge, London, 1935.

[72] T. Hayter: *Aid as Imperialism*, Penguin, London, 1971.

[73] G. M. Heal: *The Theory of Economic Planning*, North Holland, Amsterdam, 1973.

[74] J. Healey and C. Clift: 'The Development Rationale for Aid Re-Examined', *ODI Review*, No. 2, 1980.

[75] P. D. Henderson: 'Survival, Development and the Report of the Brandt Commission', *The World Economy*, June 1980.

[76] P. D. Henderson and D. Lal: 'UNCTAD IV, The Commodities Problem and International Economic Reform', *ODI Review*, No. 2, 1976.

[77] J. R. Hicks: *Causality in Economics*, Blackwells, Oxford, 1979.

[78] A. O. Hirschman: *The Strategy of Economic Development*, Yale, 1958.

[79] A. O. Hirschman: *Essays in Trespassing – Economics to Politics to Beyond*, Cambridge, 1981.

[80]   H. Hughes and J. Waelbroeck: 'Can Developing-Country Exports Keep Growing in the 1980s?', *The World Economy*, June 1981; reprinted in World Bank Reprint Series No. 194.

[81]   ILO: *Sharing in Development*, ILO, Geneva, 1974.

[82]   ILO: *Employment, Growth and Basic Needs*, ILO, Geneva, 1976.

[83]   ILO: *Poverty and Landlessness in Rural Asia*, ILO, Geneva, 1977.

[84]   ILO: *Export Led Industrialisation and Employment*, Proceedings of a Symposium, ILO, ARTEP, Bangkok, 1980.

[85]   P. Isenman: 'Basic Needs: The Case of Sri Lanka', *World Development*, March 1980.

[86]   H. G. Johnson: 'Optimal Trade Intervention in the Presence of Domestic Distortions', in R. Baldwin *et al.* (eds.): *Trade, Growth and the Balance of Payments*, Chicago, 1965.

[87]   H. G. Johnson: *Economic Policies Towards Less Developed Countries*, The Brookings Institution, Washington DC, 1967.

[88]   B. F. Johnston and P. Kilby: *Agriculture and Structural Transformation*, Oxford, 1975.

[89]   C. H. C. Kao *et al.:* 'Disguised Unemployment in Agriculture', in C. K. Eicher and L. Witt (eds.), *Agriculture in Economic Development*, McGraw Hill, New York, 1964.

[90]   D. B. Keesing and Martin Wolf: *Textile Quotas Against Developing Countries*, Thames Essays No. 23, Trade Policy Research Centre, London, 1980.

[91]   J. M. Keynes: *The End of Laissez-Faire*, Hogarth Press, London, 1926.

[92]   T. Killick: *Development Economics in Action*, Heinemann, London, 1978.

[93]   K. W. Kim: 'South Korea', in C. Saunders (ed.), *The Political Economy of New and Old Industrial Countries*, Butterworth, 1981.

[94]   I. B. Kravis: 'Trade as a Handmaiden of Growth – Similarities Between the 19th and 20th Centuries', *Economic Journal*, December 1970.

[95]   Raj Krishna: 'Farm Supply Response in India-Pakistan', *Economic Journal*, September 1963.

[96]   J. Krishnamurty: 'Changes in the Composition of the Working Force in Manufacturing 1901–51: A Theoretical and Empirical Analysis', *The Indian Economic and Social History Review*, March 1967.

[97]   A. O. Krueger: 'The Political Economy of the Rent Seeking Society', *American Economic Review*, June 1974.

[98]   A. O. Krueger: *Liberalization Attempts and Consequences*, National Bureau of Economic Research, New York, 1978. There are case studies of India, Turkey, the Philippines, South Korea, Chile, Columbia Egypt, Ghana, Israel, and Brazil in this NBER series, and Bhagwati [24].

[99]   D. Kumar and J. Krishnamurty: 'The Evolution of Labour Markets in India, 1857–1947', mimeo, Studies in Employment and Rural Development No. 72, World Bank, Washington DC, September 1981.

[100] D. Lal: 'When is Foreign Borrowing Desirable?', *Bulletin of the Oxford University Institute of Statistics*, August 1971.

[101] D. Lal: 'The Foreign Exchange Bottleneck Revisited: A Geometric Note', *Economic Development and Cultural Change*, July 1972.

[102]   D. Lal: *Wells and Welfare – An Exploratory Cost-Benefit Study of the Economics of Small-Scale Irrigation in Maharashtra'*, OECD Development Centre, Paris, 1972.

[103]   D. Lal: *Methods of Project Analysis – A Review*, Johns Hopkins, Baltimore, 1974.

[104]   D. Lal. *et al.: Appraising Foreign Investment in Developing Countries*, Heinemann, London, 1975.

[105]   D. Lal: 'Distribution and Development – A Review Article', *World Development*, Vol. 4, No. 9, 1976.

[106]   D. Lal: 'Supply Price and Surplus Labour – Some Indian Evidence'. *World Development*, Vol. 4, Nos. 10–11, 1976.

[107]   D. Lal: 'Estimates of Shadow Prices for Korea', mimeo, Discussion Papers in Public Economics No. 10, University College, London.

[108]   D. Lal: *Poverty, Power and Prejudice – the North–South Confrontation*, Fabian Research Series No. 340, Fabian Society, London, December 1978.

[109]   D. Lal: *Men or Machines*, ILO, Geneva, 1978.

[110]   D. Lal: 'The Evaluation of Capital Inflows', *Industry and Development*, No. 1, 1978; reprinted in World Bank Reprint Series No.84.

[111]   D. Lal: 'On the Multinationals', *ODI Review*, No. 2, 1978.

[112]   D. Lal: *Market Access for Semi-Manufactures from Developing Countries*, Commercial Policy Issues No. 5, Leiden for the Graduate Institute for International Studies, Geneva, and Trade Policy Research Centre, London, 1979; reprinted in World Bank Reprint Series No. 130.

[113]   D. Lal: 'Theories of Industrial Wage Structures: A Review', *Indian Journal of Industrial Relations*, Vol. 15, No. 2, 1979; reprinted in World Bank Reprint Series No. 142.

[114] D. Lal: 'The Basic Needs Approach and the Third Development Decade', mimeo, paper for the Dutch government, NAR Seminar on 'The Basic Needs Approach', The Hague, 24 July 1978.

[115] D. Lal: *A Liberal International Economic Order: The International Monetary System and Economic Development*, Princeton Essays in International Finance No. 139, Princeton, October 1980.

[116] D. Lal: *Prices for Planning – Towards the Reform of Indian Planning*, Heinemann, London, 1980.

[117] D. Lal: 'Public Enterprises', in J. Cody, H. Hughes, and D. Wall (eds.), *Policies for Industrial Progress*, Oxford University Press, 1980.

[118] D. Lal: *Resurrection of the Pauper-Labour Argument*, Thames Essays No. 28, Trade Policy Research Centre, London, 1981.

[119] D. Lal: *Cultural Stability and Economic Stagnation – India c. 1500 BC–1980 AD*, mimeo, draft manuscript, London, 1981.

[120] S. Lall: *Developing Countries in the International Economy*, Macmillan, 1981.

[121] O. Lange: 'On the Economic Theory of Socialism', *Review of Economic Studies*, 1936.

[122] Hal B. Lary: *Imports of Manufactures from Less Developed Countries*, NBER, New York, 1968.

[123] C. W. Lawson: 'The Decline in World Export Instability', *Oxford Bulletin of Economics and Statistics*, February 1974.

[124] W. Leontief: *The Structure of the American Economy*, Oxford, 1941.

[125] A. P. Lerner: *The Economics of Control*, Macmillan, London, 1946.

[126] W. A. Lewis: 'Economic Development with Unlimited Supplies of Labour', *Manchester School*, May 1954; reprinted in Agarwala and Singh (eds.) [3].

[127] W. A. Lewis: *Aspects of Tropical Trade, 1883–1965*, Almquist and Wiksell, Stockholm, 1969.

[128] W. A. Lewis (ed.): *Tropical Development 1880–1913 – Studies in Economic Progress*, Allen and Unwin, London, 1970.

[129] W. A. Lewis: *The Evolution of the International Economic Order*, Princeton, 1977.

[130] W. A. Lewis: *Growth and Fluctuations, 1870–1913*, Allen and Unwin, London, 1978.

[131] W. A. Lewis: 'The Slowing Down of the Engine of Growth', *American Economic Review*, September 1980.

[132] R. Lidman and R. J. Domerese: 'India', in W. A. Lewis (ed.) [128].

[133] R. G. Lipsey and K. Lancaster: 'The General Theory of the Second Best', *Review of Economic Studies*, Vol. 26, 1956–57.

[134] R. E. Lipsey: *Price and Quantity Trends in the Foreign Trade of the United States*, Princeton, 1963.

[135] I. M. D. Little: *A Critique of Welfare Economics*, Oxford, 1950.

[136] I. M. D. Little: 'On Measuring the Value of Private Direct Overseas Investment', in G. Ranis (ed.), *The Gap Between Rich and Poor Nations*, Macmillan, London, 1972.

[137] I. M. D. Little: 'The Developing Countries and the International Order', in R. P. Amacher, G. Haberler, and T. D. Willett (eds.): *Challenges to a Liberal International Economic Order*, American Enterprise Institute, Washington DC, 1979.

[138] I. M. D. Little: 'The Experience and Causes of Rapid

Labour-Intensive Development in Kenya, Taiwan, Turkey and Singapore: And the Possibilities of Emulation', ILO Working Paper WPII-1, ARTEP, ILO, Bangkok, 1979.

[139] I. M. D. Little: 'An Economic Reconnaissance', in Galenson (ed.) [59].

[140] I. M. D. Little: *Economic Development – Theory, Policies and International Relations*, Basic Books, New York, 1982.

[141] I. M. D. Little: 'Indian Industrialisation, 1857–1947', in M. Gersowitz *et al.*, *The Theory and Experience of Economic Development – Essays in Honour of Sir W. Arthur Lewis*, Allen and Unwin, London, 1982.

[142] I. M. D. Little and J. A. Mirrlees: *Manual of Industrial Project Analysis, Vol. II: Social Cost-Benefit Analysis*, OECD Development Centre, Paris, 1969.

[143] I. M. D. Little and J. A. Mirrlees: *Project Appraisal and Planning for Developing Countries*, Heinemann, London, 1974.

[144] I. M. D. Little and J. A. Mirrlees: 'A Reply to Some Criticisms of the OECD Manual', *Bulletin of the Oxford University Institute of Statistics*, February 1972.

[145] I. M. D. Little, Tibor Scitovsky, and Maurice Scott: *Industry and Trade in Some Developing Countries*, Oxford University Press, 1970. There are separate case studies of India, Pakistan, Brazil, Mexico, the Philippines, and Taiwan in this OECD series, all published by the Oxford University Press.

[146] T. N. Madan: 'Review of Asian Drama', *Economic and Political Weekly*, February 1969.

[147] A. Maddison: *Class Structure and Economic Growth – India and Pakistan Since the Moghuls*, Allen and Unwin, 1971.

[148] J. E. Meade: *Trade and Welfare*, Oxford University Press, London, 1955.

[149] R. I. McKinnon: 'Foreign Exchange Constraints in Economic Development', *Economic Journal*, June 1964.

[150] R. I. McKinnon: 'Financial Repression and the Liberalisation Problem Within Less Developed Countries', in S. Grassman and E. Lundberg (eds.) [60].

[151] R. I. McKinnon and D. J. Matheison: How *to Manage a Repressed Economy*, Princeton Essays in International Finance No. 145, Princeton, December 1981.

[152] G. Meier: *Leading Issues in Development Economics*, Oxford, 1964.

[153] G. Meier (ed.): *Leading Issues in Economic Development*, Oxford, 1970.

[154] G. Meier (ed.): *Leading Issues in Economic Development*, Oxford, 1976.

[155] R. F. Miksell and J. E. Zinser: 'The Nature of the Savings Function in Developing Countries – A Survey of the Theoretical and Empirical Literature', *Journal of Economic Literature*, March 1973.

[156] L. von Mises: 'Economic Calculation in the Socialist Commonwealth', in F. A. Hayek (ed.) [71].

[157] D. Morawetz: *Twenty-Five Years of Economic Development: 1950 to 1975*, World Bank, Washington DC, 1977.

[158] D. Morawetz: 'Elasticities of Substitution in Industry: What do we Learn from Econometric Estimates?', *World Development*, January 1976.

[159] Morris D. Morris: 'Private Investment on the Indian Subcontinent, 1900–1939, Some Methodological Considerations', *Modern Asian Studies*, Vol. 8, October 1974.

[160]   D. Murray: 'Export Earnings Instability: Price, Quantity, Supply, Demand?', *Economic Development and Cultural Change*, October 1978.

[161]   H. Myint: 'Economic Theory and Development Policy', *Economica*, May 1967, reprinted in Meier (ed.) [153].

[162]   G. Myrdal: *Economic Theory and Underdeveloped Regions*, Vora and Co., Bombay, 1958. (This is an expanded version of his 1956 Bank of Cairo lectures entitled: *Development and Underdevelopment – A Note on the Mechanism of National and International Economic Inequality*.)

[163]   G. Myrdal: *Asian Drama*, Penguin Books, 1968.

[164]   Dharm Narain: *The Impact of Price Movements on Areas Under Selected Crops in India, 1900–39*, Cambridge, 1965.

[165]   A. Nove: *The Soviet Economy*, Allen and Unwin, 1961.

[166]   J. Nugent and P. Yotopoulos: *Economics of Development: Empirical Investigations*, Harper and Row, New York, 1976.

[167]   R. Nurkse: *Problems of Capital Formation in Underdeveloped Countries*, Oxford, 1953.

[168]   R. Nurkse: *Equilibrium and Growth in the World Economy*, Harvard University Press, 1961.

[169]   R. O'Brien: 'Role of the Euromarket and the IMF in Financing Developing Countries', in T. Killick (ed.), *Adjustment and Financing in the Developing World*, IMF, Washington DC, 1982.

[170]   G. Papanek: 'The Effects of Aid and Other Resource Transfers on Savings and Growth in Less Developed Countries', *Economic Journal*, September 1972.

[171]   R. Prebisch: *The Economic Development of Latin America and Its Principal Problems*, United Nations, New York, 1950.

[172] R. Prebisch: 'Commercial Policy in Underdeveloped Countries', *American Economic Review*, May 1959.

[173] V. K. R. V. Rao: 'Investment, Income and the Multiplier in an Underdeveloped Economy', *Indian Economic Review*, February 1952; reprinted in Agarwala and Singh (eds.) [3].

[174] R. K. Ray: *Industrialisation in India – Growth and Conflict in the Private Sector 1914–47*, Oxford University Press, Delhi, 1979.

[175] J. Reidl: 'Lewis on Trade as the Engine of Growth in Developing Countries: What Fuels the Engine?', mimeo, Johns Hopkins University, October 1981.

[176] G. L. Reuber *et al.: Private Foreign Investment in Development*, Oxford, 1973.

[177] P. N. Rosenstein-Rodan: 'Problems of Industrialisation of Eastern and South-Eastern Europe', *Economic Journal*, June–September 1943.

[178] M. R. Rosenzweig: 'Rural Wages, Labour Supply and Land Reform: A Theoretical and Empirical Analysis', *American Economic Review*, 1978.

[179] V. Ruttan: 'The Green Revolution: Some Generalisations', *International Development Review*, Vol. XIX, No. 4, 1977.

[180] P. A. Samuelson: 'Illogic of Neo-Marxian Doctrine of Unequal Exchange', in D. A. Belsey, E. J. Kane, P. A. Samuelson, R. M. Solow (eds.), *Inflation, Trade and Taxes*, Ohio State University Press, 1976.

[181] T. Schultz: *Transforming Traditional Agriculture*, Yale, 1964.

[182] T. Schultz (ed.): *Distortions in Agricultural Incentives*, Indiana, 1978.

[183] J. A. Schumpeter: *A History of Economic Analysis*, Oxford, 1959.

[184] T. Scitovsky: 'Two Concepts of External Economics', *Journal of Political Economy*, April 1954.

[185] M. F. G. Scott, D. M. Newberry, and J. A. MacArthur: *Project Appraisal in Practice*, Heinemann, London, 1976.

[186] D. Seers: 'The Limitations of the Special Case', *Bulletin of the Oxford University Institute of Economics and Statistics*, May 1963, reprinted in Meier (ed.) [153].

[187] A. K. Sen: 'Peasants and Dualism, With and Without Surplus Labour', *Journal of Political Economy*, 1966.

[188] A. K. Sen: *Employment, Technology and Development*, Oxford, 1975.

[189] A. K. Sen: 'Personal Utilities and Public Judgments: Or What's Wrong With Welfare Economics?', *Economic Journal*, September 1979; Comment by Y. K. Ng and Reply by Sen in *Economic Journal*, June 1981.

[190] A. K. Sen: 'The Welfare Basis of Real Income Comparisons – A Survey', *Journal of Economic Literature*, March 1979.

[191] A. K. Sen: 'Public Action and the Quality of Life in Developing Countries', *Oxford Bulletin of Economics and Statistics*, November 1981.

[192] H. Singer: 'The Distribution of Gains Between Borrowing and Investing Countries', *American Economic Review*, May 1950.

[193] I. J. Singh: *Small Farmers and the Landless in South Asia*, World Bank Publication, forthcoming.

[194] Sheila Smith: 'The Ideas of Samir Amin: Theory or Tautology?', *Journal of Development Studies*, October 1980.

[195] J. Spraos: 'The Statistical Debate on the Net Barter Terms of Trade Between Primary Commodities and Manufactures', *Economic Journal*, March 1980.

[196] L. Squire: *Employment Policy in Developing Countries – A Survey of Issues and Evidence*, Oxford, 1981.

[197] T. N. Srinivasan: 'Development, Poverty, and Basic Human Needs: Some Issues', *Food Research Institute Studies*, XVI, 2, 1977.

[198] F. Stewart: 'Technology and Employment in Less Developed Countries', *World Development*, 1974.

[199] F. Stewart: *Technology and Underdevelopment*, Macmillan, 1977.

[200] F. Stewart and P. Streeten: 'Little–Mirrlees Methods and Project Appraisal', *Oxford Bulletin of Economics and Statistics*, February 1972.

[201] F. Stewart and P. Streeten: 'New Strategies for Development: Poverty, Income Distribution and Growth', *Oxford Economic Papers*, March 1976; reprinted as Chapter 8 in Streeten [204].

[202] P. Streeten: *The Frontiers of Development Studies*, Macmillan, 1972.

[203] P. Streeten: 'Changing Perceptions of Development', *Finance and Development*, September 1977.

[204] P. Streeten: *Development Perspectives*, Macmillan, 1981.

[205] P. Streeten and J. Burki: 'Basic Needs: Some Issues', *World Development*, Vol. 6, No. 3, 1978.

[206] P. Streeten and S. Lall: *Foreign Investment, Transnationals and Developing Countries*, Macmillan, 1977.

[207] Daniel and Alice Thorner: *Land and Labour in India*, Asia, Bombay, 1962.

[208] J. Tinbergen: *Statistical Testing of Business-Cycle Theories I: A Method and Its Application to Investment Activity*, League of Nations, Geneva, 1939.

[209] R. Vernon: *Sovereignty at Bay*, Basic Books, New York, 1971.

[210] J. Viner: *International Trade and Economic Development*, Oxford, 1953.

[211] B. Warren: 'Imperialism and Capitalist Accumulation', *New Left Review*, September–October 1973.

[212] T. E. Weisskopf: 'The Impact of Foreign Capital Inflow on Domestic Savings in Underdeveloped Economies', *Journal of International Economics*, February 1972.

[213] World Bank: *Accelerated Development in Sub-Saharan Africa*, Oxford University Press, 1981.

[214] World Bank: *World Development Report 1982*, Oxford University Press, 1982.

[215] World Bank: *IDA in Retrospect*, Oxford University Press, 1982.

POSTSCRIPT 1997

Introduction

This small book provided an interpretative survey of the ideas and events which influenced development policies, particularly those concerning trade and industrialisation, in the first three decades after World War II. Its general theme was the rise of the *Dirigiste Dogma*, whose fall has been the most remarkable event since it was written. In its updating, it is useful, therefore, to set the remarkable events of the last decade – which have seemingly ushered in a new Age of Reform – in broad historical perspective.

Since the French Revolution, six phases in the evolution of the global economy can be identified after the mercantilist system broke down because of its internal contradictions.[1] The *first* was the great liberal international economic order (LIEO) created under British leadership after the repeal of the corn laws in 1846. The next 20 years were the heyday of world-wide free trade. This period also saw the development of the intellectual justification for this order in Ricardo's famous law of comparative advantage.

With the rise of protectionism in the US and Germany in the 1860s and 1870s, new arguments for protection also arose

---

1   See Heckscher (1955), Lal-Myint (1996) for these contradictions, and the latter for the similarities in the causes of the breakdown of the neo-mercantilist systems created in the Third World.

associated with the names of Hamilton and List. This *second* period of creeping protectionism, and the scramble for empire, culminated in World War I. It was during these first two phases that much of the Third World was integrated into the world economy, and many of them began their own process of modern economic growth which has been identified as a sustained rise in *per capita* income.[2]

The *third* period from 1913 to 1950, encompassing two world wars and the Great Depression, can be looked upon as one in which the 19th-century international trading and payments system, which had transmitted the growth impulse around the world, broke down. It led in turn – as we have seen in this book – to the inward-looking policies most of the Third World adopted in the *fourth* of our periods, which spans the end of World War II and the first oil price shock of 1973.

During this post-war golden age – whose course was charted in earlier chapters – except for a few small countries on the Pacific Rim, most developing countries did not emulate the developed countries which gradually liberalised the controls on foreign trade and payments they had instituted during the inter-war period. But the example of the New-Industrialised Countries, the disappointing results of their past *dirigisme*, and the process of dealing with the multiple shocks in the volatile global economy ushered in by the OPEC coup in the 1970s led in the *fifth* period (covering the 1970s and much of the 1980s) to an intermittent but gradual movement away in most of the Third World from 'inward' to 'outward' looking policies.

---

2   See Reynolds (1985).

This marks the beginning of the latest (*sixth*) period. The collapse of the Second World in 1989 accentuated this trend towards liberalisation. The global economy has at last taken off from when it broke down – first slowly and then cataclysmically during the late 19th and the first half of the 20th century. But there is one important difference. Whereas under the 19th-century liberal free trade order there was global free movement of goods, capital *and* labour, the new liberal free trade environment does not encompass the last – given the ubiquitousness of immigration controls. This is in part due to the fears in the West of being swamped by the unwashed, unlettered and coloured poor of the Third World, and in part because of the incentives seemingly provided by Western welfare states for such migration. It is this cultural and political resistance rather than any economic argument[3] which ensures that there is little prospect of restoring this aspect of the 19th-century free trade order.

In this Postscript I briefly chart this breathtaking world-wide movement from the plan to the market, as well as providing some guide to the current and emerging debates on development.

The overall trends

Figures A1 and A2 present a succinct picture of the relative economic performance of developing and OECD countries in the post-war period, as judged by their respective rates of growth of *per capita* output. Since the 1970s, these growth rates (despite the relatively higher population growth rates in the Third World)

---

3   See Barry and Goodin (1992) for the political and cultural arguments and Simon (1991) for the economic ones concerning free movement of people.

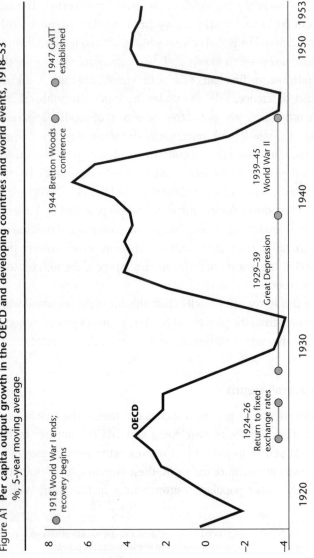

Figure A1 Per capita output growth in the OECD and developing countries and world events, 1918–53

%, 5-year moving average

- 1918 World War I ends; recovery begins
- 1924–26 Return to fixed exchange rates
- 1929–39 Great Depression
- 1939–45 World War II
- 1944 Bretton Woods conference
- 1947 GATT established

OECD

Source: World Bank, *World Development Report 1991*, p. 17.

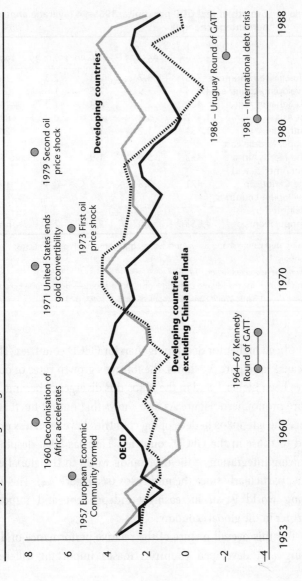

Figure A2 **Per capita output growth in the OECD and developing countries and world events, 1953–88**
%, 5-year moving average

1957 European Economic Community formed

1960 Decolonisation of Africa accelerates

1971 United States ends gold convertibility

1973 First oil price shock

1979 Second oil price shock

Developing countries

OECD

Developing countries excluding China and India

1964-67 Kennedy Round of GATT

1986 – Uruguay Round of GATT

1981 – International debt crisis

1953   1960   1970   1980   1988

8
6
4
2
0
-2
-4

Source: World Bank, *World Development Report 1991*, p. 17.

Table A1 **Growth of real GDP per capita, 1965–94 (average annual percentage change)**

Group	Population, 1989 millions	1965–73	1973–80	1980–89	1990–94[b]
Industrialised countries	773	3.7	2.3	2.3	1.0
Developing countries	4,053	3.9	2.5	1.6	0.2
Sub-Saharan Africa	480	2.1	0.4	−1.2	−1.8
East Asia	1,552	5.3	4.9	6.2	8.0
South Asia	1,131	1.2	1.7	3.0	2.0
Europe, Middle East and North Africa	433	5.8	1.9	0.4	−0.5[c]
Latin America and the Caribbean	421	3.8	2.5	−0.4	1.8
Developing countries weighted by population[a]	4,053	3.0	2.4	2.9	n/a

a Using population shares as weights when aggregating GDP growth across countries.

b *World Development Report, 1996*.

c This figure is for the Middle East and North Africa and does not include Europe.

Source: World Bank: *World Bank Development Report, 1991*, p. 3.

have been higher for developing than for OECD countries. This is because, as Figure A3 shows, the former's growth rates of output have been higher – and in the 1980s this divergence became even more pronounced. Figure A3 also shows that output fluctuations since the late 1980s in developing countries have been less closely tied to those in the OECD countries. This has been despite the growing integration of the developing world in the global economy, particularly since the mid-1980s (see Figure A4). The developing world is an increasingly independent and important partner in the global economy.

But this overall picture of the relative performance of developing and developed countries masks important differences

Figure A3 **Developing and industrial countries: output growth, 1953–2000[a]**
%

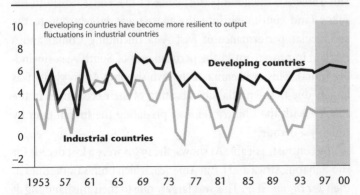

a Prior to 1970, growth in industrial and developing countries is based on a subset of countries for which data are available from *International Financial Statistics*. Shaded area indicates IMF staff projections.
Source: IMF, *World Economic Outlook*, October 1995, p. 44.

Figure A4 **Developing and industrial countries: openness, 1970–94[a]**
% of GDP

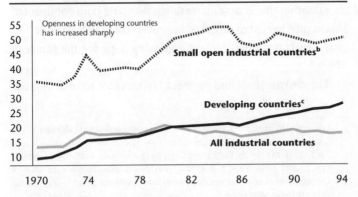

a Average of exports and imports of goods and services as a % of GDP.
b Belgium, Denmark, the Netherlands and Sweden.
c Excludes oil-exporting countries.
Source: IMF, *World Economic Outlook*, October 1995, p. 44.

209

within the Third World. As can be seen from Figures A1 and A2, and Table A1, the good performance of the Third World in the 1980s (and continuing into the 1990s) was largely due to the spectacular performance of East Asia (including China) and a marked improvement in the performance of South Asia (including India). This awakening of the two sleeping Asian giants was largely due to the partial liberalisation of their economies in the 1980s – with the Chinese reforms predating the Indian ones by roughly a decade.[4]

By contrast, as Table A1 shows, the 1980s were a lost decade for sub-Saharan Africa and Latin America, which both saw declines in their *per capita* GDP. This was largely due to their mishandling of the shocks set in motion by the first oil price shock of 1973.[5] The world economy has since been subjected to a roller-coaster ride of commodity prices and real interest rates. The so-called debt crisis which mainly afflicted these two regions was a symptom of this failure of past *dirigisme*. But it also provided the impetus for the liberalisation that is now increasingly sweeping both continents.[6] This in turn has led to a marked improvement in economic performance in Latin America,[7] and a growing hope for the future in Africa.[8]

The *dirigiste* trade and payment régimes that were ubiquitous

---

4　I provide a comparative account of reforms in both countries in Lal (1995), which also contains extensive references.

5　See Celb (1988), Bevan, Collier and Cunning (1989, 1990), Collier and Gunning (1994, 1995). Deaton and Miller (1995) provide a detailed econometric study of the macro-economic performance in sub-Saharan Africa in the face of volatile primary commodity prices.

6　See Lal (1987), Sachs (1988), Little *et al.* (1993), Lal-Myint (1996).

7　See Edwards (1995).

8　See World Bank (1994).

Figure A5 **Growth of world real GDP and world trade growth, 1970–96**
% of GDP

The cyclical recovery has boosted the growth of world output and trade above trend,
while inflation in the industrial countries remains contained.

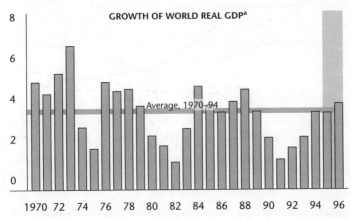

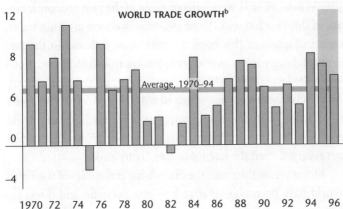

a Shaded area indicates IMF staff predictions.
b Goods and services, volume.
Source: IMF, *World Economic Outlook*, October 1995, p. 1.

211

Figure A6 **Share of exports in GDP, selected country groups, 1900–86**
%

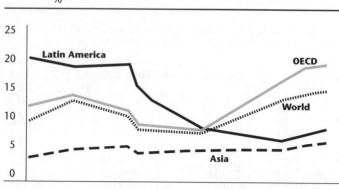

Note: Export share in GDP can be viewed as a proxy for integration. GDP data are in international dollars; exports in US dollars.
Source: World Bank, *World Bank Development Report, 1991*, p. 17.

after World War II were a major cause of the past economic failure of the Third World. These deleterious effects are outlined in earlier chapters of this book. Despite some setbacks in the late 1970s and early 1980s, world trade has continued to boom: growing in the late 1980s and 1990s at twice the rate of world output. Asia's relative success as compared with Latin America has been in part due to its increasing integration in this booming world economy. By contrast, Latin America's growing 'inwardness' was not reversed until the late 1970s (see Figure A6).

Moreover, in the 1990s the liberalising economies of the Third World have been able to attract private portfolio and direct investment (in contrast with the more risky syndicated bank borrowings of the 1970s). Thus, except for Africa, private flows of foreign capital are now of greater importance than the official 'aid' flows on which so much passionate ink has been spilt in the past (Figure A7).

But, as Table A2 shows, the bulk of investment which is the essential fuel for growth continues to be provided by domestic savings. These differences in savings rates and thence in the rate of investment and the efficiency with which it is deployed continue to be the major proximate causes for differences in growth rates of output and thence the relative economic performance of countries. Moreover, it is differences in policy regimes which in large part account for the differences in both the level and efficiency of investment.[9]

Events and ideas

In this updating, we need to take up the story of events and ideas impinging on development policy from the late 1970s. A good starting point is the first oil price shock which brought the post-war golden age to an end, and whose early effects are discussed in previous chapters of the book. Through the reactions it promoted, it also led to the final breakdown of the *Dirigiste Dogma* in the Third World. But before that, the actions of OPEC were hailed by many in the Third World as showing the route towards 'commodity power', and how a massive transfer of resources from rich to poor countries could be effected. Demands for a new international economic order (NIEO) – a world planned economy entailing massive international redistribution of income – were born.[10]

---

9   This is the conclusion of the 21-country comparative study of Lal-Myint (1996) based on the economic histories of these countries during the 1950–85 period.

10   See Lal (1994), Ch. 4.

213

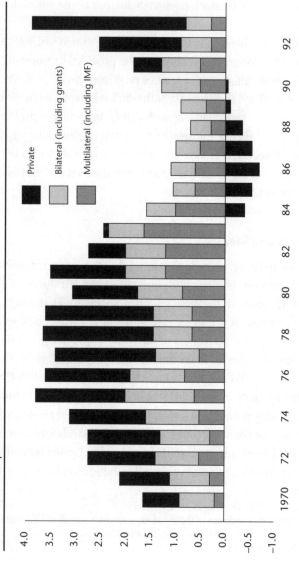

Figure A7 Net flows to developing countries, 1970–93
% of recipient GNP

Private

Bilateral (including grants)

Multilateral (including IMF)

Source: M. Bruno and B. Pleskovic (eds), *Annual World Bank Conference on Development Economics 1995*, p. 170.

Commodity power

It has been known since J. S. Mill that, if a country has some mono-poly or monopsony power in its foreign trade, then in the absence of foreign retaliation, it can garner more of the cosmopolitan gains from trade by levying the so-called optimum tariff to turn the terms of trade in its favour. This is what the OPEC cartel in effect did. Many other developing countries sought to do the same. Commodity power seemed to be the new Third World weapon in its ongoing skirmishes with the West.

But, as Alfred Marshall had noted, even if the short-term elas-ticities of demand and supply for many traded goods are low, they will be much higher in the long run. Oil proved this case. The mas-sive rise in its price promoted successful substitution through var-ious conservation measures, and increased the returns to exploration – so that known reserves rose. Compared with oil, both the short- and long-run elasticities of demand and supply for most other primary commodities were even higher. So nothing came of commodity power – its death-knell being pronounced by the decline in the real price of oil in the 1980s.[11]

An enduring myth that had fuelled the NIEO, and the program for raising the prices of commodities formulated by UNCTAD, was the belief that the terms of trade between pri-mary commodities and manufactures would inexorably de-cline.[12] Basing themselves on past export structures, this was translated into an inexorable tendency for the terms of trade of

---

11 McBean (1966) is the major pioneering study which questioned the adverse ef-fects on growth of commodity price and export earnings instability. Newberry and Stiglitz (1981) is a thorough analysis of UNCTAD's proposal for a Common Fund for commodities.

12 The seminal contributions are Singer and Prebisch as noted in the main text.

Table A2 Investment and saving, 1965–94, % of GDP

Economy group	Gross domestic investment				Foreign savings				Gross national savings			
	1965–73	1974–80	1981–89	1994	1965–73	1974–80	1981–89	1994	1965–73	1974–80	1981–89	1994[b]
Low income	19.6	24.4	26.4	30	1.2	1.1	3.4	2	18.4	23.3	23.0	28
China	24.8	31.0	34.9	42	-0.3	-0.1	5.5	-2	25.2	31.1	34.4	44
India	17.1	21.3	23.9	23	1.7	1.1	3.6	2	15.3	20.3	20.4	21
Indonesia	13.7	23.6	29.5	29	2.6	-3.0	2.7	-1	11.1	26.7	26.9	30
Kenya	21.0	24.1	23.7	21	4.4	8.9	7.1	-3	16.6	15.2	16.6	24
Nigeria	14.1	22.2	12.0	10	4.3	-1.3	2.7	-1	9.7	23.5	9.3	11
Low income[a]	14.1	19.6	19.1	17	2.8	2.3	6.2	6	11.3	17.2	12.9	11
Middle income	21.6	26.4	23.2	26	3.0	5.3	3.4	1	18.1	21.0	19.7	25
Brazil	20.5	23.8	19.8	21	1.9	4.6	1.8	-1	18.5	19.2	18.0	22
S. Korea	23.3	30.0	29.8	38	8.2	7.1	0.8	-1	15.1	22.9	29.0	39
Morocco	14.3	26.0	24.4	21	2.7	14.5	13.0	5	11.7	11.5	11.4	16
Malaysia	21.2	27.3	30.7	39	-1.5	-1.2	3.3	2	22.7	28.5	27.4	37
Philippines	20.5	29.3	20.1	24	1.4	5.4	2.4	6	19.0	23.9	17.7	18
Thailand	23.9	26.6	25.8	40	2.4	5.1	4.2	5	21.5	21.5	21.6	35

a Excluding China and India.

b 1994 Figures are from the *World Development Report 1996*, and are Gross Domestic Savings.

Source: World Bank: *World Bank Development Report 1991*, p. 119.

developing countries to decline. Suffice it to say that, as far as the most relevant index, the *income* terms of trade of developing countries, is concerned there is no such tendency.[13] With the eventual collapse of most attempts at rigging international commodity markets – the latest being the demise of the International Tin Agreement – the commodities issue has hopefully been buried – at least for the time being!

The debt crisis

The 1973 OPEC price coup, however, also led to a large transfer of resources from oil-importing countries to OPEC, whose ability to absorb the resultant foreign exchange accruals in their domestic economies was limited. They had to find a home for this new-found wealth. Much of this was deposited in Western banks, particularly in their offshore subsidiaries – which formed the Eurodollar market. With the deflationary impulse transmitted by this transfer of resources from countries with low to high savings propensities, cries for recycling the OPEC surplus became clamorous. The banks obliged. The beneficiaries were Third World countries – particularly in Latin America – which had endemic problems financing their budgets. They now found a new source of borrowing and at negative real interest rates! The seeds of the debt crisis were sown.

---

13 See Grilli and Yang (1988). Cuddington (1992) provides a sophisticated time-series analysis of the trend in prices of 26 individual commodities relative to those of manufactured goods for the period 1900–83. He finds that 16 of the 26 commodity prices are trendless, five have statistically significant negative trends and the remaining five significant positive trends. He concludes that the Prebisch-Singer thesis should 'certainly not be considered a universal phenomenon or a "stylized fact"'(p. 207).

To deal with the stagflation of the 1970s deriving from the OPEC oil price rise, there was a general tightening of macro-economic policy in the West towards the end of the 1970s. The resulting slowdown in world demand and rise in world interest rates dealt a double blow to the governments of heavily indebted countries. Their borrowings had been made at floating interest rates and were in most part directly or indirectly underwritten by their governments. As real interest rates rose to unknown heights, governments needed to raise the fiscal resources and to convert them into foreign exchange to finance the large increase in debt service that ensued.

Some countries, mainly in East Asia, managed this transfer problem in textbook fashion. They were helped by the capacity of their economies to convert domestic resources into foreign exchange because of their past outward-oriented trade policies, and because they had established viable fiscal systems. Many debtors in Latin America and Africa had neither attribute. The debt crisis created an acute fiscal crisis for these states, most often reflected in acute inflation. While, given their past neglect of exports, the only way to obtain the necessary balance of trade surplus was through import compression, which in turn led to domestic recession.

The resulting debt crisis was not, as some observers claimed,[14] due to the *inability* of these countries to pay – as witness Mexico's immense oil wealth – but rather to their *unwillingness*.[15] For the debt crisis exposed the unsustainable nature of their endemic fis-

---

14 See Cline (1984).

15 As sovereign borrowers do not face any legal form of enforcement of claims on them, they will only continue to service their debt as long as the expected utility from repaying is greater than if they default. This means, as Eaton *et al.* (1986) show, that they will be unwilling to pay well before they are unable to do so.

cal deficits which the previous inflow of cheap money had concealed. These fiscal deficits, and the accompanying 'inward looking' policies, reflected the unsustainable entitlements to politically determined income streams to various favoured groups that past *dirigisme* had created. Rather than rescind these political entitlements, a softer option was to renege on their foreign debt – which in effect is what the various reschedulings of the 1980s amounted to.

It was to deal with these joint fiscal, foreign debt and balance-of-payments crises that economic liberalisation was undertaken, most often under the aegis of the World Bank and the International Monetary Fund (IMF).[16]

The real exchange rate and 'Dutch disease'

One important technical development in thinking about macroeconomic policy, which came to the fore in the 1980s, was the concept of the real exchange rate.

One consequence of the volatility of commodity prices and capital flows after the 1973 OPEC coup was that many countries received large windfalls in the form of foreign exchange – whether through larger revenues from commodity price rises, foreign aid flows, or the remittances from their nationals who found employment in the booming oil-producing countries of the Middle East. These led to an appreciation of the real exchange rate from the bonanza of foreign exchange – a phenomenon first observed when the Dutch found large reserves of natural gas. *Mutatis mutandis*, in the downturn of the cycles in commodity prices and capital flows,

---

16   See Lal (1993), Chs. 5 and 8, and Little *et al.* (1994).

219

the real exchange rate would need to depreciate. To adjust to cyclical shocks from the world economy, these required movements in the real exchange rate caused serious problems in many countries.

To see why, it is useful to outline briefly the 'Australian' model of balance-of-payments adjustment.[17] This aggregates the goods produced and consumed in an economy into two categories: traded and non-traded. The domestic prices of the former, for countries which are 'price-takers' in international markets, will be given by these foreign currency prices and the country's nominal exchange rate. The price of non-traded goods is set by domestic demand and supply. The real exchange rate[18] is defined as the domestic *relative* price of non-traded to traded goods.[19]

Suppose the economy maintains *a fixed nominal* exchange rate. It is initially in internal and external equilibrium, with domestic output equal to expenditure, and with no deficit in the current account of the balance of payments. There is then a large inflow of capital (or foreign exchange earnings from a rise in the price of its commodity exports). This will have two effects. *First*, it will allow domestic expenditure to exceed output by the amount of the inflow. *Second*, the country will have to run a current account deficit – with imports exceeding exports – by the same amount. Both effects will lead to a real exchange rate appreciation. For the excess expenditure now made possible will raise in some proportion –

---

17   Corden (1986) provides a lucid account of the mechanics of the model.

18   If e = the nominal exchange rate, p_n = the price of non-traded goods, p_f = the foreign currency price of traded goods, p_t = the domestic price of traded goods, and e_r = the real exchange rate, then by definition:

$$e_r = (p_n/p_t) = (p_n/e \cdot p_f)$$

19   Latin Americans, being upside down, define it as the inverse of this definition, viz., the ratio of traded to non-traded goods prices.

depending on preferences – the demand for both traded and non-traded goods.

The excess demand for traded goods will be readily met through imports, without any change in the domestic price of traded goods. But as the supply of non-traded goods *ex hypothesi* is purely domestic, the excess demand for them must raise their price. This will induce both an increase in their supply, and by *lowering* the relative price of traded goods also lead to a shift in consumption towards traded goods, which will be met by a further increase in imports. In the new equilibrium, the relative price of non-traded goods (the real exchange rate) will thus be permanently higher; there will be a reduction in the domestic output of traded and expansion in that of non-traded goods; and there will be a current account deficit exactly equal to the inflow. Also the price level will be higher.

But this latter effect depends crucially upon the assumed fixity of the *nominal* exchange rate. If the latter were flexible, then the required *real* exchange rate appreciation (which is an equilibrium phenomenon and hence unavoidable) could come about with a fall in the domestic price of traded goods through an *appreciation of the nominal exchange rate.*[20] There would be no need for the price of non-traded goods and hence the general price level to rise. But the relative output effects – with a shrinkage of the traded good producing sectors – must still occur. These two aspects of the Dutch disease which have been identified and observed in many countries which have received foreign currency bonanzas, or large capital inflows, are different: the shrinkage of

---

20   Thus as $e_r = p_n / e \cdot p_f$, the required rise in e_r can come about with a rise in e, with p_n and p_f unchanged.

the traded goods sector is unavoidable, but the rise in the price of non-traded goods and thence the price level is not. This depends upon what policy is followed with respect to the *nominal* exchange rate.

To see the relative merits of fixed versus flexible nominal exchange rates in adjusting to volatile capital or commodity markets, consider the case when – for whatever reason – the capital inflow or the foreign exchange bonanza ends. The country will no longer be able to finance the excess of domestic expenditure over output, and of imports over export earnings which the foreign currency inflows had previously allowed. It will have to both cut domestic expenditure and eliminate the current account deficit.

Suppose the country, by deploying suitable monetary and fiscal policies, is willing to reduce expenditure so that it equals output. But it maintains a fixed nominal exchange rate. If, for whatever reason, the *prices of non-traded goods are inflexible downwards*, or slow to adjust, then the relative price of non-traded goods (the real exchange rate) which needs to fall, will not adjust. This will prevent the required switch of domestic expenditure from traded to non-traded goods and thereby the cure for the balance-of-trade deficit. In such a case, the only way in which the requisite depreciation of the *real* exchange rate can occur is if the *nominal* exchange rate is depreciated. Without this adjustment, the expenditure reduction required to achieve balance-of-payments equilibrium must lead to a domestic recession with unemployment.

There is considerable evidence that misalignment of real exchange rates due to inappropriate nominal exchange rate policies was part of the problem which led to the painful adjustment many Latin American and African countries had to make in dealing with their debt crises in the 1980s.[21, 22] In an increasingly integrated world economy with global capital markets moving huge sums at the press of a button, flexibility of the nominal exchange rate becomes an important means of insulating the economy from the volatility of capital flows and commodity prices.

The revival of classical political economy

The structural adjustments (World Bank) and stabilisation (IMF) programs adopted to deal with the 1980s 'debt crisis' increasingly embodied the intellectual consensus that was emerging at the beginning of the decade in favour of markets against the plan. The final nail in the coffin of the 'old' development economics was the realisation, both in theory and practice, of the immense corruption that a system of controls engenders.

Although some forms of corruption – which are a form of arbitrage, albeit illegal – aid efficiency, the unproductive scramble for the valuable licences on which the Permit Raj was based, led to additional losses of economic welfare. Thus, an import quota, for example, is a gift by the government of a licence to print money to

---

21 Many countries, particularly those in the Southern Cone of Latin America, also tried to use the nominal exchange rate as an anchor to lower inflationary expectations, as part of the stabilisation programmes they instituted to deal with chronic or hyper-inflation. The most common form was the 'tablita', or a pre-announced downward crawl of the nominal exchange rate equal to the difference between the officially desired inflation rate and the expected world rate of inflation. But most of these exchange-rate-based stabilisation programmes broke down because the underlying fiscal deficits causing inflationary pressures were not dealt with. The actual inflation rate did not fall to that desired, and the net effect was a substantial appreciation of the real exchange rate, which further worsened the balance of payments. See Little *et al.* (1993) for evidence.

22 See Edwards (1989, 1995).

the lucky beneficiary: who can tax consumers by pocketing the difference between the price at which he imports the good and the much higher domestic price at which he can sell it because of the quota restrictions. If 'rent seekers' compete for these quota rents, in aggregate they will spend an amount equal to the total rent to be derived, in the form of resources of time and money – waiting in queues, lobbying, bribery, and so on. Thus in addition to the loss suffered by consumers from the rise in the price of the good, there will be a deadweight loss equal to the whole of the quota rents – as if the equivalent resources had been dumped into the sea![23]

But once it is recognised that, with the politicisation of economic life, *dirigisme* necessarily breeds rent-seeking, with its attendant costs, then many of the prescriptions of so-called 'public economics' – which supposedly provides the grammar of arguments for rational public intervention – also fall by the wayside.

We have seen how the modern theory of trade and welfare argues for maintaining free trade but abandoning *laissez-faire*. It recommends dealing with various domestic distortions through domestic taxes and subsidies. But domestic subsidies – providing politicised income streams – will be subject to rent seeking as much as tariffs and quotas. In that case the twin classical prescriptions of free trade and *laissez-faire* seem the only workable ones to promote economic development.[24]

But as the classical economists were the first to point out, this does not imply the promotion of anarchy or a neutered state. As Mill stated clearly in the textbook whose policy prescription remained the orthodoxy for half a century, the state has to provide

---

23   The seminal articles are Tullock (1967) and Krueger (1974).
21   See Lal (1994a).

the essential public goods – law and order, defence, a sound currency – partially finance various merit goods for the needy – education (possibly health), and a social safety net to alleviate the poverty of the 'deserving poor'. Beyond that, economic activities are best left to private agents. This is very much the consensual policy package of the 1990s for promoting economic development.

These classical prescriptions were based both on economics and an understanding of the eternal dilemmas of politics. The most important change in thinking on economic policy in the Third World has been the recognition that the assumptions about the nature of the state that underpinned planning are unrealistic. It was implicitly assumed that the state was benevolent, omniscient and omnipotent. As we saw in Chapter 4, outside Communist countries, any belief about the last of these attributes was quickly shattered; their omniscience was increasingly doubted as planners showed a lack of foresight which would have swiftly bankrupted a private agent. But the assumption that the State – whether democratic or authoritarian – is a committee of benevolent Platonic Guardians has been more tenacious.

A more clear-headed appraisal of the motives of the State arose with the resurrection of the ideas of the classical economists associated with the Scottish Enlightenment – particularly David Hume and Adam Smith – combining politics and economics (in the so-called 'new' political economy). Though there are some Platonic Guardian states or elements of it within most, many states are better viewed as being self-interested, even predatory. It is this realisation which has led to the search for a policy package subserving the interests of the prey rather than the predator. A predatory state is interested above all in discretionary resources and hence will seek to maximise its revenues. The interests of the prey are to provide only enough revenues to finance the essential public goods. How these differing ends are to be reconciled remains controversial.[25]

There is more agreement on how the past *dirigisme* of the Second and Third Worlds can be reversed. Above all, it is essential to macro-economic balance, ideally through a monetary constitution which prohibits any future levying of the inflation tax. The other components of the policy package include, *first*, the conversion of import quotas into tariff equivalents, and then a gradual movement towards a low uniform tariff, which is ultimately reduced as close to zero as possible. *Second*, the removal of price controls and all forms of industrial licensing. *Third*, the liberalisation and rationalisation of domestic capital markets – with the removal of interest rate ceilings and centrally planned direction of credit. *Fourth*, the removal of exchange controls and the maintenance of realistic exchange rates. *Fifth*, the privatisation of state enterprises, not merely on grounds of efficiency, but on those of political economy: to remove the state from areas where it has no role and to allow it to concentrate on the things only it can do.

As it is unlikely that all these reforms can be undertaken simultaneously, lively but inconclusive debate continues about the appropriate sequencing of these reforms.[26]

The political economy of reform

One lesson from past experience is, however, of importance. In the reform process time may be of the essence. This is linked to the

---

25   See Findlay (1990), Lal (1988), Chs. 13.2, and Lal (1993), Ch. 3. Bates (1988) provides a view from political science.

26   See Lal (1993), Ch. 5, Edwards (1984, 1992), Sell (1988), and Funke (1992).

question of why self-interested predatory states, who have benefitted from their past *dirigisme*, should suddenly want to liberalise and serve the general weal. Here the parallel with the liberalisation of the mercantilist 'anciens régimes' in the late 18th and 19th centuries is instructive.[27]

One unintended consequence of past mercantilism and contemporary neo-mercantilism is that, while both were motivated by the desire to establish 'order' and thence 'nations' by expanding the scope of government control, after a certain stage increased *dirigisme* bred disorder. As economic controls become onerous, people attempt to escape them through various forms of avoidance and evasion. This has a devastating effect on the state's fiscal base. The first sign of an impending crisis is fiscal, with the accompanying un-Marxian 'withering away of the State'. It is to regain control over what seem to have become ungovernable economies that economic liberalisation is undertaken, to restore the fiscal base and government control. Once this crisis of the state seems to be manageable, there is no further incentive for the predatory state to continue with liberalisation.

This suggests that a 'crisis' provides an opportunity for liberalisers – but it may be of short duration.[28] A big bang may therefore be desirable to smash the equilibrium of rent-seeking interest groups who have a stake in maintaining the past system of *dirigisme*. To stiffen the government's spine in this unenviable task,

---

27 See Heckscher (1955) for the springs of past mercantilism and Lal and Myint (1996) for the similar motives underlying contemporary neo-mercantilism.

28 I can immodestly claim to be amongst the first to have noted the importance of a 'crisis' in initiating liberalisation in Lal (1987). The hypothesis has since been widely confirmed: see Little *et al.* (1993), Lal-Myint (1996), Bruno-Easterly (1996), among others.

sweeteners which ease its fiscal problems, in the form of soft loans or grants from multilateral and bilateral foreign governments, may be desirable. Beyond that the role of foreign assistance seems limited.[29]

Whilst events as much as ideas have led to this new consensus on policy at least amongst policy-makers, there are many in the academy who have not given up their *dirigiste* attachments. We must briefly examine the more influential of these *dirigiste* ideas.

The mutations of the *dirigiste* dogma
Shifting notions of competition

In thinking about these recent attempts to provide an intellectual basis for *dirigisme*, it is useful to note the subtle but important shift that has occurred in economists' notions of competition from the classics – spanning Adam Smith to J. S. Mill – to modern mainstream economics. The latter's intellectual moorings are provided by the so called Arrow-Debreu theory of general equilibrium, which it is claimed gives precision to the claims of the classics on the virtues of the market (see Arrow and Halin, 1971). But, as Blaug (1987) points out, one needs to note:

> the subtle but nevertheless unmistakable difference in the conception of 'competition' before and after the 'marginal revolution'. The modern concept of perfect competition, conceived as a market structure in which all producers are price-takers and face perfectly elastic sales curves for their outputs, was born with Cournot in 1838 and is foreign to the

---

29 This is a vindication of Peter Bauer's longstanding arguments against foreign aid: see Bauer (1976, 1981). Lal (1993), Ch. 8, surveys the changing role of foreign capital in development over the last four decades.

classical conception of competition as a process of rivalry in
the search for unrealised profit opportunities, whose
outcome is uniformity in both the rate of return on capital
invested and the prices of identical goods and services but
not because producers are incapable of making prices. In
other words, despite a steady tendency throughout the
history of economic thought to place the accent on the
end-state of competitive equilibrium rather than the process
of disequilibrium adjustments leading up to it, this
emphasis became remorseless after 1870 or thereabouts,
whereas the much looser conception of 'free competition'
with free but not instantaneous entry to industries is in
evidence in the work of Smith, Ricardo, Mill, Marx and of
course Marshall and modern Austrians. For that reason, if
for no other, it can be misleading to label classical
economics as a species of general equilibrium theory except
in the innocuous sense of an awareness that 'everything
depends on everything else' (p. 443).

It is equally surprising that the 'Chicago school', as Kirzner
(1994) for instance has noted,

> maintains that the competitive market economy displays
> systematic regularities only to the extent that it can be
> reasonably fitted into the perfectly competitive mold.
> Subsequent [to Frank Knight] generations of Chicago
> theorists would maintain that as a matter of fact the real
> world competitive market *can* so be fitted (p. 103).

Thus we are now in the situation where most theorists on both
sides of the market-*dirigiste* divide use the Arrow-Debreu model as
their paradigm.

From this theoretical perspective the two so-called Fundamental Theorems of Welfare Economics are derived, which theo-

rists (for example, Dasgupta, 1980, Hahn, 1984, Sen, 1983) assert provide the justification for the superiority of a market economy. Whilst if one or the other condition for the existence of the Utopian state of perfect competition is not met, there is 'market failure' and thence a *prima facie* case for government intervention. This as Chapter 1 argued is bizarre. For it is child's play to show that because of incomplete markets, external effects and the existence of public goods, 'market failure' defined as deviations from the perfectly competitive norm is ubiquitous. But the corollary that this then requires massive corrective public action is highly dubious, to say the least.

This was also the intellectual basis of the planning syndrome, as we noted in surveying the famous debate between Lange, Lerner, von Mises and Hayek in the 1930s, in Chapter 4. However, as Hayek rightly insisted, planning was infeasible because the market-based price mechanism is essential as it makes use of the division of knowledge which is unavoidable in any real-world economy.

The failures of centralised planning are now well known – with the events of 1989 having hopefully buried the planning syndrome. For even our theorists[30] accept that the major cause for 'incomplete' markets is imperfect information, which causes problems of what is called 'incentive compatibility' – exactly the point made by Hayek and von Mises in the 1930s. Thus a command economy on Lange-Lerner 'market socialist' lines is ruled out.

---

30   See Greenwald and Stiglitz (1986), Dasgupta (1980), Stiglitz (1995).

Neo-classical public economics

But now the hope is held out that a full optimum or Pareto improvements can be achieved by the government implementing a system of optimal taxes and subsidies. This 'optimal tax' basis for the 'new' *dirigisme* is set out in Stiglitz (1995), and its theoretical base is claimed to be the working out of this optimal tax structure in Greenwald and Stiglitz (1986). Its relevance is, however, strictly limited *first*, because its implementation raises questions about the character of the mandarins required to implement these 'optimal taxes', and *second*, because in a dynamic economy the optimal structure will have to be continually changing and the requisite information will not be readily available to the authorities – as Hayek (1945) noted a long time ago.[31]

On the first question concerning political economy, Greenwald and Stiglitz (1986) note in a footnote:

> It might be noted that we ignore any discussion of the
> political processes by which the tax-subsidy schemes
> described below might be effected. Critics may claim that as
> a result we have not really shown that a Pareto
> improvement is actually possible. (note 7, p. 234)

---

31 Newbery and Stern (1987) have advocated the application of this optimal tax theory to developing countries. But as they note, it assumes that 'the government has coherent, unified and largely benevolent objectives, captured in the social welfare function, and we search for ways in which the tools available to it can be used to improve the measure of welfare' (p. 653). That the theory is irrelevant for most developing countries is patently obvious as most of their policies do not even come close to these assumptions about their character. Whilst if a predatory state or rent-seeking society is accepted as likely, the optimal tax rules are no longer valid even within this framework (see Lal (1994), Ch. 13). For a trenchant critique of optimal tax theory see Harberger (1987), who moreover notes that it is based on a philosophy of government – the social engineering view – which differs from that of classical liberalism.

Quite!

Whilst on their claim

that there exist Pareto-improving government interventions ... [and] that the kind of intervention required can be simply related to certain parameters that, in principle, are observable. (p. 23 1),

they are in their concluding comments forced to concede:

we have considered relatively simple models, in which there is usually a single distortion (one kind of information imperfection, one kind of market failure). Though the basic qualitative proposition, that markets are constrained Pareto efficient, would obviously remain in a more general formulation, the simplicity of the policy prescriptions would disappear. Does this make our analysis of little policy relevance? The same objection can, of course, be raised against standard optimal tax theory. (Some critics might say, so much the worse for both.) (p. 258).

Quite!

To those of us who spent our misspent youth on advocating the second-best shadow pricing Little-Mirrlees rules which were the precursors of this 'new' *dirigisme*, its policy irrelevance is hardly surprising.[32]

'New' growth and trade theories

The other 'new' theories of: (a) endogenous growth (Romer, 1986,

---

32 See Lal (1980) for one of these exercises in irrelevance, and Lal (1993), Chapter 1, how I came to eschew this 'public economics' approach to public policy.

Lucas, 1988) and (b) trade in the presence of monopolistic competition (Brander and Spencer, 1984; Helpman and Krugman, 1985) which are being touted as providing justifications for *dirigisme* can be dealt with more summarily.

The 'new' growth theory is driven by the valid desire to repair a major defect of the neo-classical growth model (due to Solow and Swan), namely that in it the steady state rate of growth of output of the economy is determined entirely by the exogenous factors of population growth and technical progress. Thus, the level of investment and its efficiency, which all the evidence suggests are the mainsprings of growth, only affect the *level* of the steady state *per capita* income but not its *rate* of growth. The 'new' growth theorists seek to endogenise the role of investment in growth by claiming that there are externalities to human capital or knowledge, or there are increasing returns to investment.

We need only note that neither theorists (see Solow, Stern, 1991) nor practitioners (see Pack, 1994) have found it persuasive. In its so-called AK version it is a reversion to the Harrod-Domar model,[33] whilst there is little evidence to support the purported

---

33 Thus if g = growth rate of output (Y); s = the ratio of savings to national income (S/Y); k = the capital-output ratio (K/Y); n = the growth rate of the labour force (L), the Harrod-Domar equation for steady state growth is:

$$g = s/k = n \quad (1)$$

In the neo-classical model, with constant returns to scale, the production function is:

$$Y = Af(K,L) \quad (2)$$

where A is total factor productivity. This yields the well-known growth accounting identity:

$$g = t + a \cdot (dK/K) + b \cdot n \quad (3)$$

where t = rate of technical progress; a and b are the elasticities of output with respect to capital and labour. In the constant returns, Cobb-Douglas case a + b = 1. With perfect competition a and b will also be the share in income of capital and labour. Since in the steady state dK/K = g, from (3) the determinants of steady

n capital and 'knowledge' as asserted by its
-Myint, 1996).

al departure in endogenising the role of invest-
has been made by Scott, who makes three depar-
ne Solow-Swan framework. *First,* he argues that
depr   n is essentially a transfer of income from capitalists to
workers in a progressive economy. Were the 'appreciation' (in
workers' income) which results not excluded, as it is in conventional national income accounting, then 'net' investment for society as a whole is (approximately) equal to gross investment as
conventionally measured and not to gross investment minus depreciation. *Second,* he argues that there are no diminishing returns
to cumulative gross investment, but there could be diminishing returns to the *rate* of investment. Third, he argues that there is no
need to invoke any independent or exogenous technical progress
to explain growth. Defining investment as the cost of change
means that all activities (including technical progress) associated

---

state *per capita* growth rates are:

$$g - n = [t + n(a + b - l)]/(1 - a) \quad (4)$$

with constant returns to scale $a + b = 1$, *per capita* growth rates are entirely determined by the exogenous factors t and n. Endogenous growth theorists have
shown that even without increasing returns to scale ($a + b > 1$) there can be positive *per capita* income growth if there are constant returns to capital ($a = 1$) and
with ($t = O$) non-reproducible labour is assumed away, because it is argued that
what is important for growth is not the numbers working but the human capital
embodied in them. If all these reproducible inputs are put into a composite good
called 'capital', then the production function becomes:

$$Y = AK^a \quad (5)$$

The growth accounting equation from this is:

$$g = t + a(dK/K)$$

with strict constant returns to capital ($a = 1$) – a mathematical requisite to present
explosive growth – and no technical progress ($t = O$), this reduces to the Harrod-
Domar identity: $g = s/k$, as $dK/K = [(dK/Y)/(Y/K)] = [(I/Y)/(Y/K)]$.

with growth are covered by it. Hence in his model there is only change (growth) due to investment and to population growth. He provides a detailed empirical analysis which shows that the growth experience of developed countries conforms to his model, whilst Lal-Myint find that it also provides a good statistical fit for the growth experience of the 25 developing countries we studied.

The 'new' growth theory has also spawned a whole new industry estimating cross-country regressions based on the data compiled by Heston and Summers. Apart from the fragility of the inferences which can be drawn on their basis,[34] these statistical exercises have at best established that, statistically, growth rates are determined by good policy.[35] But the regressions themselves cannot conclusively establish what these policies are![36] The Lal-Myint study by examining the economic history of 25 developing countries whilst endorsing the role of good policy in determining the efficiency of investment, which more than its volume is found to be the major proximate cause for the differences in growth rates, also

---

34 See Levine and Renelt (1992).

35 Barro (1994), Sala-Martin (1994).

36 These regressions have also addressed one seeming anomaly. The neo-classical growth model predicts that there should be convergence of growth rates across countries, with richer countries with larger *per capita* capital stocks growing more slowly than poorer ones with smaller amounts of capital per head. Whilst such convergence does appear to characterise the experience of developed countries, that of developing countries appears to be marked by a divergence of growth rates. The notion of 'conditional convergence' introduced by Barro is useful in clearing up this anomaly. Each country is now seen as approaching its own particular target of steady state income *per capita* (yi^*) which is determined not only by a common global technology, but by country-specific political and cultural factors. An economy will then grow faster if its initial income per head (yi) is further away from its target steady state level (yi^*). Barro finds that for the 114 countries in the Summers-Heston data set there is such conditional convergence of *per capita* income at the rate of 1.5% per annum, which is close to the rate of convergence he finds for the states of the US and the regions of Europe and Japan.

identifies these policies. They echo the classical prescriptions, and now form what has been termed the 'Washington consensus' on economic policy by John Williamson (1990).

The 'new' trade theory has been neatly encapsulated by Baldwin (1992) in the traditional framework of trade and welfare outlined in earlier chapters.[37] This shows that part of the 'new' trade theory's case for intervention is another variant of the classic terms-of-trade type argument for trade intervention and another part is a variant of the infant industry argument for the domestic promotion of industry (but not its protection). As the practical irrelevance of both types of arguments have been discussed threadbare in the trade and welfare literature, these 'new' arguments for protection and industrial policy are once again mere theoretical curiosa.

Market governance or business governance?

By contrast, many have found the case studies of supposedly successful *dirigisme* in the Far East conducted by the self-proclaimed 'market governance' school more persuasive. Even the World Bank (1993) has leaned towards them. Wade (1990) and Amsden (1989) are the more audacious, taking the prime exhibits (Taiwan and Korea) in the 'outward oriented' cupboard and converting them into shining[38] examples of successful *dirigiste* trade and industrial policies.

---

37 Baldwin (1992) shows how it can be geometrically incorporated into a refurbished 'Baldwin envelope'.

38 There is an ongoing statistical debate about how to define 'openness', and to use such statistical measure to provide econometric evidence in support of the thesis that openness promotes growth. For a survey of this equivocal literature see Edwards (1993), Lal (1994), Ch. 7.

Detailed critiques are available elsewhere.[39] I need only emphasise a number of points.

First, it is undeniable that these governments were *dirigiste* in many aspects of their trade and industrial policies. The question remains whether their undoubted success was due to or despite this *dirigisme*. Little (1994), basing himself on estimates of social rates of return to investment for Korea (for which he had data), shows convincingly that they were inversely correlated with the degree of *dirigisme*. Whilst the World Bank *Miracle* study's empirics based on total factor productivity calculations, despite its circumlocutions, found that interventions in both Korea and Taiwan had little effect in altering the structure of production at the sectoral level, and that the least selective intervention in these and other Asian miracle economics – the commitment to manufactured exports – was the most successful. Thus despite the claims of the 'market governance' school these economies vindicate policies of 'getting prices right' rather than of getting them wrong!

Second, another more persuasive explanation can be provided for their industrial and trade policies.[40] Following some insights

---

39 See Little (1994), Lal (1994), Ch. 7. It should however be noted that the past comparative studies of numerous developing countries' trade and industrial policies showed that changes in policy which affect a country's participation in international trade affect its economic performance. Studies (for instance, Wade) which argue that protection was rife even in the NIC's are therefore beside the point. For the past comparative studies merely establish that reducing the degree of protection raised the rate of growth of the relevant country. From this one can infer that the neo-classical theory of trade and welfare is of relevance for developing countries, and that moving to free trade would lead to an even higher rate of growth, as the theory predicts. But as, apart from Hong Kong – now extinguished – there is no entirely free-trading nation, there can be no conclusive empirical evidence to confirm this inference.

40 See Lal (1994), Ch. 7.

of Demsetz (1988) concerning the problem of control of business enterprises I have suggested that what these and other countries were concerned with was dealing with this problem as their industrial structure moved beyond the relatively labour-intensive end of their ladders of comparative advantage. The problem is one of maintaining 'beneficial control over resources in the presence of economies of size ... [which is related to the amount of private] wealth required to reduce the degree to which ownership is separated from control of these resources' (Demsetz, 1995). This agency problem arises as countries effectuate their emerging comparative advantage in more capital-intensive and *ipso facto* larger-scale enterprises.

Three ways have been used in developing countries to overcome this agency problem. The *first* is through sufficient concentration of private wealth, and some institutional means for its spread over a number of enterprises while maintaining control by some concentrated owners. The *second* is through public enterprises. The *third* is through foreign equity controlling local firms.

Korea, following Japan, sought to create concentrations of private wealth through the promotion of the 'chaebol'. The provision of long-term subsidised credit to a select number of industrial groups was the major policy instrument. The select firms were 'chosen' by a relatively efficient dynamic monitoring process based on export success – under a relatively neutral overall trade régime. But the resulting concentration of economic power has subsequently become a political albatross.

In Taiwan, by contrast, as the Kuomintang government was concerned with the political consequences of promoting native Taiwanese economic power, it chose the public sector route for capital-intensive industries like ship-building and petrochemicals, but with the usual damage to efficiency and profitability.[41]

Finally, Singapore chose the third route. But its 'neutral' trade régime ensured that the direct foreign investment was not of the 'tariff jumping' kind, and hence likely to be both socially as well as privately profitable.[42]

Then there is the 'laissez-faire' example of Hong Kong. Whilst Singapore did try to force the pace at which its industries were to move up the ladder of comparative advantage (with some dire results as in the 1980s recession) Hong Kong let its industrial structure evolve more naturally. If performance is judged by the productivity of capital then Hong Kong has been the more successful.[43]

A counter-counter-revolution in development theory?

This suggests that there is little merit in the 'new' *dirigiste* case. So why has Krugman (1992) proclaimed a 'counter-counter-revolution in development theory'? Because he claims the ideas of the old development economics based on the importance of increasing returns, and pecuniary external economies arising from the effects of market size, which underwrote concepts like the 'big push' and 'backward and forward linkages', have now been formalised and shown to be logically consistent. He claims the reason why it failed to persuade in its earlier incarnation was because of the failure to formalise the ideas in mathematics. But this is ridiculous. As his discussant Stiglitz (1994) rightly noted: 'That we can write down a

---

41 See Wade (1990), p. 81.

42 See Lal (1975) for case studies of the social costs and benefits of direct foreign investment in countries with trade protection.

43 See Findlay-Wellisz (1993); Lal-Myint (1996); Young (1992).

model of a phenomenon proves almost nothing. It does not make the idea right or wrong, important or unimportant' (p. 1). The reasons why ideas like the 'big push' and 'linkages' do not persuade were clearly set out in the detailed discussion by Little (1982). Murphy *et al.*'s (1989) writing down a formal model does not in itself validate a big push which depends upon the income effects associated with increasing returns – which are irrelevant in any real open economy.

Moreover, we now have empirical evidence of the outcomes in countries which did try a big push. Four were included in the Lal-Myint study – Ghana and Madagascar in Africa, Brazil and Mexico.[44] The results invariably were disappointing if not disastrous (as in Ghana and Madagascar). To promote such bad policies just because some theorists have been able to write down some algebra is not only puerile but wicked – given the high costs that the poor people thus being experimented on suffer.

New horizons
Good governance

But it is still an open question whether, once a market economy is established, it can be maintained against the unavoidable political pressures for its subversion. The sad fate of many constitutions shows how fragile a corset they are in constraining a predatory state. A political culture which internalises the classical liberal virtues may be a better bulwark. Questions concerning the appropriate institutions which help to create and foster the requisite character and culture have therefore, come to the fore of the current debates on development.

---

44   Also see Lal and Maxfield (1993) for a detailed analysis of the Brazilian case.

As it is human to think that one's own 'habits of the heart' are ideal, it is not surprising that the West is now seeking to promote Western democracy in the Third World as the means of ensuring the good governance now generally recognised to be a prerequisite for economic development. Whatever the moral virtues of democracy, the historical evidence does not support any necessary connection between this form of government and the promotion of prosperity.[45] Even in the rocky transition from the plan to the market, as the contrasting experiences of Russia and China show, glasnost may not help perestroika![46]

The characteristics of good government are more important than its particular form. On this issue the classical liberals (Hume and Smith) remain relevant. Whilst upholding benevolence as the

---

45 De Tocqueville is as usual both prescient and succinct: 'It is very true,' he writes in *The Ancien Régime* (Fontana, London, 1971): 'that in the long run liberty always leads those who know how to keep it to comfort, well-being, often to riches: but there are times when it impedes the attainment of such goals; and other times when despotism alone can momentarily guarantee their enjoyment. Men who take up liberty for its material rewards, then, have never kept it for long ... What in all times has attracted some men so strongly to liberty has been itself alone, its own peculiar charm, independent of the benefits it brings; the pleasure of being able to speak, act, and breathe without constraint, under no other rule but that of God and Law. Who seeks in liberty something other than itself is born to be a slave.' (p. 217)

46 There has recently been a flurry of interest in trying to examine if there is some statistical link between democracy and growth. The most sophisticated of these is by Helliwell which also reviews earlier studies. But the statistical proxies for the political variables used in these exercises do not inspire much confidence. Also see Deaton and Miller (1995), who rightly note that these exercises are plagued by the econometric problem of identification. 'In the absence of some influence from outside the political and economic system of each country, these political economy models remain essentially unidentified, the best they can do is to demonstrate that it is possible to use the data to tell one story or another' (p. 73). It should also be noted that in the Lal-Myint comparative study of the economic histories of 25 developing countries no link was found between democracy and growth.

primary virtue, they also recognised its scarcity. But fortunately, as Smith showed, a market economy which promotes 'opulence' does not depend on this virtue for its functioning. It only requires a vast number of people, even without personal relationships, to deal and live together without violating the 'laws of justice'. The resulting commercial society promotes some virtues – hard work, prudence, thrift – which as they benefit the agent rather than others are inferior to altruism. But as unintentionally these lower-level virtues do help others through their promotion of general prosperity, the resulting society is neither immoral nor amoral. Thus a good government is one which promotes 'opulence' through a policy of preserving 'natural liberty' by establishing laws of justice which guarantee free exchange and peaceful competition, the improvement of morality being left to institutions outside the government. It would be inappropriate for the state to legislate morality.

This classical liberal view of *civil association*, with the state as the custodian of laws which do not seek to impose any preferred pattern of ends (including abstractions such as the general welfare, or fundamental rights), but which merely facilitate individuals to pursue their own ends, has been challenged by a rival conception of society as an *enterprise association*. The state is now seen as the manager of an enterprise seeking to use the law for its own substantive purposes, and in particular for the legislation of morality. As the British philosopher, Michael Oakeshott, has shown, both conceptions of the state have deep roots in Western thought, going back to ancient Greece in one case and the Judaeo-Christian tradition in the other.[47]

It is important to note that socialism is the major secular em-

---

47   See Oakeshott (1975, 1993).

bodiment of society viewed as an enterprise association: with its desire to use the state's power to equalise people. The demise of the socialist economies does not mean this socialist impulse is dead, least of all in the First World. It continues to infect the design of an appropriate social safety net to protect the 'poor'. In combination with democratic politics it remains a continuing threat to the sustainability of a market order, and to the classical liberal view of civil society.[48]

Welfare states for the Third World?

It is not surprising, therefore, that with the seeming victory of the market over the plan, the *dirigiste* bands have consolidated under the banner of 'adjustment with a human face'.[49] They now seek to create Western-style welfare states in the Third and Second worlds.[50]

48 The growing environmental movement with its slogan of 'sustainable development' is also part of this renewed *dirigiste* backlash. An adequate treatment of this new face of *dirigisme* is beyond the scope of this book, but I have dealt with it in Lal (1994) Ch. 4, and Lal (1995). Also see Beckerman (1995), Ridley (1995), Balling Jr. (1992).

49 UNICEF is the progenitor of this slogan. Their case is set out in Cornia, Jolly and Stewart (1987). See Behrman (1991) for a more balanced discussion of issues relating to nutrition, health and development. He does not find their case convincing and concludes: 'in fact the underlying studies seem to be characterized better as reflecting how well societies and people have adapted to minimize negative health and nutrition effects rather than the more negative interpretation given by UNICEF'(p. 152).

50 It is worth noting that an important objective that many socialists have set for the welfare state is redistributive egalitarianism. However, as classical liberals have maintained, egalitarianism is not a universally accepted creed, despite the gallons of ink spent by so many philosophers to justify their prejudices as the dictate of reason. Recently Sen (1992) has claimed that classical liberals are also egalitarians with respect to the good 'liberty'. But as Sugden argues convincingly, this is a misreading of the classical liberal position which cannot be subsumed, as Sen suggests, into a theory of the social good.

In assessing their claims it is useful to make two distinctions. The first is between *extensive* and *intensive* growth. *Extensive* growth has occurred for millennia in most parts of the world with aggregate output rising, *pari passu*, with the expansion of population that has taken place since our ancestors came down from the trees. *Per capita* income was, however, relatively low and stagnant during this phase. By contrast the modern era has been marked by intensive growth with a secular rise in *per capita* incomes as the growth of output outstripped that of population. There has been a two centuries dispute whether such rises in *per capita* income will alleviate poverty – that is, whether the fruits of intensive growth will 'trickle down' and alleviate poverty.

In answering this question it is useful to distinguish between three types of poverty, based on their causes. These are mass structural poverty, destitution and conjunctural poverty. It is worth noting that though this distinction was well known in the past – for instance in discussions of the English poor law since Elizabethan times – one strategic linguistic move by socialists was to conflate all of them, so that structural poverty – about which nothing could be done until the era of modern growth – was conflated with destitution – for whose relief most societies have adopted remedial measures.[51]

Mass structural poverty has for most of history been mankind's natural state. For, until recently, most economies were

---

51 A similar confusion for instance surrounds the whole recent discussion by a distinguished theorist of what he calls An Enquiry into Well-Being and Destitution (Dasgupta, 1993). What he is discussing is mass structural poverty reflected for instance in malnutrition and ill-health, which though ubiquitous in the past – and more widespread than it need be in India today – is different from true destitution. For critiques see Srinivasan (1994) and Subramanian and Deaton (1996).

agricultural economies, or what the economic historian E. A. Wrigley has called 'organic' economies, whose growth was ultimately bounded by the productivity of land. In such an economy there is a universal dependence on organic raw materials for food, clothing, housing and fuel. Their supply is in the long run inevitably constrained by the fixed factor – land. This was also true of traditional industry and transportation – depending on animal muscle for mechanical energy, and upon charcoal (a vegetable substance) for smelting and working crude ores and providing heat. Thus in an organic economy once the land frontier has been reached, diminishing returns will take their inexorable toll. No wonder the classical economists were so gloomy. With diminishing returns to land, conjoined to the Malthusian principle of population, a long-run stationary state where the mass of people languished at a subsistence standard of living seemed inevitable. Thus whilst there could be some extensive growth with both population and output growing at about the same rate – leaving a relatively constant level of *per capita* income – till the land frontier was reached; thereafter, the only remedy to prevent immiserisation was some form of population control.

But even in an organic economy there was some hope of getting intensive growth – which leads to a secular increase in *per capita* incomes. The system of market 'capitalism' and free trade outlined and defended by Adam Smith could increase somewhat the productivity of an organic economy over what it was under mercantilism, and also by lowering the cost of the consumption bundle, would lead to a rise in *per capita* income – that is, intensive growth. But if this growth in popular opulence led to excessive breeding, the land constraint would inexorably lead back to subsistence wages. Technical progress could hold the stationary state at bay but the land constraint would ultimately take hold.

The Industrial Revolution led to the substitution of this organic economy by a mineral-based energy economy. Coal and the steam engine allowed virtually unlimited supplies of mechanical energy. Intensive growth now became possible, as the land constraint on the raw materials required for raising aggregate output was removed. Thus the Industrial Revolution in England was based on two forms of 'capitalism', one institutional, namely that defended by Adam Smith because of its productivity-enhancing effects, even in an organic economy – and the other physical: the capital stock of stored energy represented by the fossil fuels which allowed mankind to create in the words of E. A. Wrigley:

> a world that no longer follows the rhythm of the sun and the
> seasons; a world in which the fortunes of men depend
> largely upon how he himself regulates the economy and not
> upon the vagaries of weather and harvest; a world in which
> poverty has become an optional state rather than a
> reflection of the necessary limitations of human productive
> powers. (Wrigley, 1988, p. 6)

Not only the subsequent experience of the First, but of many countries in the Third World has borne this out. It is possible, as many countries in East Asia for instance have shown, to eradicate mass poverty within a generation, because neither of the twin foundations of the gloomy classical prognostications, diminishing returns, nor the Malthusian principle are any longer secure. A market-based liberal economic order which promotes labour-intensive growth can cure the age-long problem of structural mass poverty.[52]

---

52 See Lal-Myint (1996) for the empirical evidence and in particular Fields (1991).

The *dirigistes*, however, would have us believe that without the establishment of Western-style welfare states – the so-called 'direct' route to poverty alleviation – poverty in the conflated sense which also incorporates destitution and conjunctural poverty cannot be cured.[53] Whatever the economic merits of this view, it raises serious problems of political economy.

For the Western welfare state is itself in trouble because of the dynamic costs associated with its inevitable enlargement in majoritarian democracies. Under factional pressures, politicians bid for votes by offering transfers of income to some chapters of the populace at the expense of others. With the inevitable 'universalisation' of benefits, the welfare state comes to be captured by the middle classes with a tendency for *net* transfers of income from both the rich and the poor to the middle income groups. The same tendency is observed in those developing countries (Uruguay, Costa Rica, Sri Lanka, Jamaica) which, under the factional pressures of majoritarian democracy, created and expanded their welfare states.[54] These were financed by taxing the rents from their major primary products. With the expansion of revenues during upturns in the primary product price cycle, political pressures led to their commitment to entitlement which could not be repudiated when revenues fell during the downturn. The ensuing increase in the tax burden on the productive primary product sector – to close the fiscal gap – led to a retardation of its growth and productivity, and in some cases to the 'killing of the goose that laid the golden egg'.

Similar fiscal pressures have also attended the universalisation

---

53   The UNDP's Human Development Reports are the major outlet for these views.
54   See Lal and Myint (1996).

of benefits in Western economies.[55] With political entitlement (mainly pensions and health care) whose fiscal burden is governed more by demography than the conjunctural state of the economy, the growing tax burden creates well-known distortions that discourage productivity and growth.[56] The reform of the welfare state is therefore at the forefront of public policy debates in the First World, just when many are seeking to establish or expand them in the Third!

Nevertheless, ways to deal with the poverty caused by the inevitable vagaries of life, over the life cycle of some individuals (conjunctural poverty), and of the persistent poverty of those of nature's victims who are incapable of earning a living (destitution), have been recognised by many classical liberals to be part of the state's functions. No ideal means are available to achieve this end.

Ideally the benefits should be targeted. But, apart from the well-known problems this creates in terms of perverse incentives for the 'able-bodied' poor, there will also be a tendency for them to be made universal in democracies. It is not surprising therefore that the most efficient poverty-redressal programs in the Third World were instituted in Pinochet's Chile and Lee Kwan Yew's Singapore.[57]

To overcome problems of moral hazard, adverse selection and monitoring in relation to income transfers, there is revived inter-

---

55   See Lal (1994), Ch. 15, which also provides detailed references to the relevant literature.

56   Lal and Wijnbergen (1985) provide a model in which the demographically determined social expenditures in developed countries lead to structural fiscal deficits which crowd out investment in developing countries through linkages in the global capital market. Also see Lal and Wolf (1986).

57   See Castaneda (1992), Findlay and Wellisz (1993).

est in using private associations (on the lines of the 19th-century U.K.'s mutual aid friendly societies) for dealing with poverty caused by risks which could in principle be insured against.[58] The task of dealing with the 'deserving poor' is devolved to private charities – whose funds are possibly supplemented from the public purse on a matching basis. This use or creation of non-governmental organisations (NGOs) to deal with the intractable problems of low-end poverty can also be seen as a way of restoring civil association, from the inevitable depredations it has suffered at the hands of proponents of the state seen as an enterprise association in the name of alleviating poverty.[59]

But this current flurry of interest in decentralising and privatising many of the tasks the state (seen as an enterprise) has taken on itself, must also be viewed with caution. For historically, one of the major NGOs involved in alleviating poverty has been the Church. But whether in its Judaeo-Christian or Islamic form, these monotheistic, revelatory religious institutions have been at odds with the liberal notion of civil association. These churches have themselves been enterprise associations, which every so often have also sought to convert the state into one (a theocracy). It is debatable whether friends of the market should seek to strengthen an institution through public subsidy, which historically has been – and in some cases continues to be – an enemy of the market. But there may be a case for using more secular NGOs in servicing the poor.

---

58   See Green (1993).
59   See Lal (1994b).

Culture and development

No form of government or agency for promoting good government can thus be taken as granted to be ideal. Ultimately, these forms are likely to be less important than the existing habits of a people (including those which might evolve with modernisation and industrialisation). But these relate to questions of character and culture.[60] It is by no means self-evident, as the previous discussion has emphasised, that Western democracy necessarily promotes a culture which is market-friendly. Its uneasy tension between the rival notions of the State seen as a civil or enterprise association, can lead to a form of decadence in private habits – which some have identified as a feature of many contemporary Western societies. With the substitution of public for private benevolence, the transfer state saps the latter – the highest private moral virtue for classical liberals, while every turn towards making the State an enterprise association saps those lower-level 'vigorous virtues'[61] – productivity, thrift, and self-reliance – which classical liberals see as underpinning the market and thence the promotion of 'opulence'.

But once the religious roots of the Western impulse towards creating a state as an enterprise association are recognised, it is evident that there are other non-Semitic religions, which have never sought to legislate morality. Hinduism and Confucianism, for instance, are ways of life (cultures rather than religions), without the centralised institutions of the various Christian or Islamic churches, seeking to capture the State to serve their own substantive ends. They can, as they have, provide the cultural sustenance

---

60 See North (1990) for a robust defence of the argument that culture and the institutions it generates matter.

61 This term is due to Shirley Letwin (1992).

for promoting the vigorous virtues, and unlike their Semitic counterparts, may not subvert the state seen as a civil association. Where the plan has replaced the market in the countries of these cultures, it is because the State was captured by elites infected with the secular Western virus which views the State as an enterprise – whether it be Fabian socialism in India, or Marxism in China.

In conclusion, therefore, once it is realised that it is Western culture and Western forms of government which themselves have had this uneasy tension between the state seen as a civil or enterprise association, mirrored in the pendular swings from market to plan to market, it is evident that the mere transfer of Western forms of governance and their attendant ideology is as unlikely to secure the market in the Third World as it is in the First. It would be sheer arrogance to deny that there may be other cultures, which may be equally or even more compatible with that Western classical liberal vision of the State as a civil association, which provides the general political underpinning, but not necessarily a particular form of government, for the perpetuation of the market.

Beyond this little can be said, for with the increasing compartmentalisation of the social sciences in the 20th century, the type of speculations and research on the grand themes of culture and development, undertaken by 19th-century social scientists like de Tocqueville and Max Weber, has sadly atrophied. A revival of this grand tradition is a precondition for thinking sensibly about these unsettled questions concerning economic transformation and development.[62]

---

62 My own attempt at this is contained in the Ohlin lectures I delivered in 1995 – see Lal (1998).

REFERENCES FOR 1997 POSTSCRIPT

Amsden, A. H. (1989): *Asia's Next Giant*, New York: Oxford University Press.

Arrow, K. J. and F. H. Hahn (1971): *General Competitive Analysis*, San Francisco: Holden-Day.

Baldwin, R. E. (1992): 'Are Economists' traditional policy views still valid?', *Journal of Economic Literature*, Vol. 30, June, pp. 804–29.

Balling Jr., R. C. (1992): *The Heated Debate: greenhouse predictions versus climate reality*, San Francisco: Pacific Research Institute for Public Policy.

Barro, R. J. (1991): 'Economic Growth in a cross-section of countries', *Quarterly Journal of Economics*, Vol. 106, May, pp. 407–43.

Barro, R. J. (1994): 'Economic Growth and Convergence', *Occasional Paper* No. 46, San Francisco: International Center for Economic Growth.

Barry, B. and R. E. Goodin (eds.) (1992): *Free Movement*, Hemel Hempstead, Herts.: Wheatsheaf.

Bates, R. (ed.) (1988): *Towards a Political Economy of Development*, Berkeley CA: University of California Press.

Bauer, P. (1981): *Equality, the Third World and Economic Delusion*, London: Weidenfeld & Nicolson, 1987.

Bauer, P. (1976): *Dissent on Development*, revised edn., Cambridge, MA: Harvard University Press.

Beckerman, W. (1995): *Small is Stupid*, London: Duckworth.

Behrman, J. R. (1991): 'Nutrition, Health and Development', in G. Psacharopoulos (ed.), *Essays on Poverty, Equity, and Growth*, Oxford: Pergamon Press.

Bevan, D., Paul Collier and Jan Gunning (1989): *Peasants and Governments: An Economic Analysis*, Oxford: Clarendon Press.

Bevan, D., Paul Collier and Jan Gunning (1990): *Controlled Open Economies*, Oxford: Clarendon Press.

Blaug, M. (1987): 'Classical Economics', in Eatwell, Milgate, Newman (eds.), *The New Palgrave – A Dictionary of Economics*, Vol.1, London: Macmillan.

Brander, J. A. and B. J. Spencer (1984): 'Tariff Protection and Imperfect Competition', in H. Kierzkiwski (ed.), *Monopolistic Competition and International Trade*, Oxford: Clarendon Press.

Bruno, M. and W. Easterly (1996): 'Inflation's Children: Tales of Crises that Beget Reforms', *NBER Working Paper No. 5452*, February, Cambridge, Mass.: NBER.

Castaneda, T. (1992): *Combating Poverty*, International Center for Economic Growth, San Francisco, CA: ICS Press.

Cline, W P. (1984) *International Debt: Systematic Risk and Policy Response*, Washington D.C.: Institute for International Economics.

Collier, P. and J. Gunning (1994): *Trade Shocks: Consequences and Policy Responses in Developing Countries*, International Center for Economic Growth, San Francisco, CA: ICS Press.

Collier, P. and J. Gunning and associates (1995): *Trade Shocks in Developing Countries*, Oxford: Oxford University Press.

Collier, P. and D. Lal (1986): *Labour and Poverty in Kenya*

1900–1980, Oxford: Clarendon Press.

Corden, W. M. (1986): *Inflation, Exchange Rates and the World Economy*, 3rd edn., Chicago: University of Chicago Press.

Cornia, G. A., R. Jolly and F. Stewart (eds.) (1987): *Adjustment with a Human Face*, Oxford: Clarendon Press.

Cuddington, J. (1992): 'Long-run Trends in 26 Primary Commodity Prices: A Disaggregated look at the Prebisch-Singer Hypothesis, *Journal of Development Economics*, Vol. 39.

Deaton, A., and R. Miller (1995): 'International Commodity Prices, Macroeconomic Performance, and Politics in Sub-Saharan Africa', *Princeton Studies in International Finance*, No. 79, December, International Finance Section, Dept. of Economics, Princeton, NJ: Princeton University.

Dasgupta, P. (1980): 'Decentralisation and Rights', *Economica*, Vol. 47, May.

Dasgupta, P. (1993): *An Enquiry into Well Being and Destitution*, Oxford: Clarendon Press.

Demsetz, H. (1995): *The Economics of the Business Firm*, Cambridge: Cambridge University Press.

Dreze, J., and A. K. Sen (1989): *Hunger and Public Action*, Oxford: Clarendon Press.

Eaton, J., M. Gersovitz and J. Stiglitz (1986): 'The Pure Theory of Country Risk', *European Economic Review*, Vol. 30, June.

Edwards, S. (1984): 'The order of liberalisation of the external sector in Developing Countries', *Essays in International Finance*, No. 156, Princeton: Princeton University Press.

Edwards, S. (1989): *Real Exchange Rates, Devaluation and Adjustment*, Cambridge, Mass.: MIT Press.

Edwards, S. (1992): *The Sequencing of Structural Adjustment and*

Stabilisation, Occasional Paper No.34, International Center for Economic Growth, San Francisco, CA: ICS Press.

Edwards, S. (1993): 'Openness, Trade Liberalization and Growth in Developing Countries', *Journal of Economic Literature*, September.

Edwards, S. (1995): *Crisis and Reform in Latin America*, New York: Oxford University Press.

Fields, G. (1991): 'Growth and Income Distribution', in G. Psacharopoulos (ed.): *Essays on Poverty, Equity and Growth*, Oxford: Pergamon Press.

Findlay, R. (1990): 'The new Political Economy: Its explanatory power for LDC's', *Economics and Politics*, Vol. 2, No. 2, pp. 93–221.

Findlay, R., and S. Wellisz (1993): *The Political Economy of Poverty, Equity and Growth: Five Small Open Economies*, New York: Oxford University Press.

Funke, N. (1992): 'Timing and Sequencing of Reforms: Competing Views', Kiel Working Paper No. 552, Kiel, Germany: Kiel Institute of World Economics.

Gelb, A. (1988): *Oil Windfalls: Blessing or Curse?*, New York: Oxford University Press.

Green, D. (1993): *Reinventing Civil Society: the rediscovery of welfare without politics*, Choice in Welfare series No. 17, IEA Health and Welfare Unit, London: Institute of Economic Affairs.

Grilli, E. R., and M. C. Yang (1988): 'Primary Commodity prices, manufactured goods prices, and the terms of trade of Developing Countries: what the long run shows', *World Bank Research Observer*, Vol. 2, No. 1, pp. 1–47.

Greenwald, B. C., and J. E. Stiglitz (1986): 'Externalities in Economies with Imperfect Information and Incomplete

Markets', *Quarterly Journal of Economics*, Vol. CI, March,
pp. 229–64.

Hahn, F. H. (1984): 'Reflections on the Invisible Hand', in his
Equilibrium and Macroeconomics, Oxford: Blackwells.

Harberger, A. C. (1987): 'Neutral Taxation', in Eatwell, Milgrom
and Newman (eds.): *The New Palgrave*, Vol. 3, London:
Macmillan.

Hayek, F. A. (ed.) (1935): *Collectivist Economic Planning*, London:
Routledge.

Hayek, F. A. (1945): 'The Use of Knowledge in Society', *American
Economic Review*, Vol. XXXV, No. 4, Sept., pp. 519–30.

Heckscher, E. (1955): *Mercantilism*, 2 vols., revised 2nd edn.,
London: Allen and Unwin.

Helliwell, J. F. (1992): 'Empirical linkages between Democracy
and Economic Growth', *NBER Working Paper No. 4066*, May,
Cambridge, Mass.: National Bureau of Economic Research.

Helpman, E. and P. Krugman (1985): *Market Structure and Foreign
Trade*, Cambridge, Mass.: MIT.

Kirzner, I. M. (1994): 'The Ethics of Competition', in H. Siebert
(ed.): *The Ethical Foundations of the Market Economy*,
Tübingen: J.C.H. Mohr, pp. 101–14.

Krueger, A. O. (1974): 'The Political Economy of the Rent-Seeking
Society', *American Economic Review*, Vol. LXIV, pp. 291–303.

Krugman, P. (1992): 'Toward a counter counter-revolution in
Development Theory', *Proceedings of the World Bank Annual
Conference on Development Economics*, pp. 15–38.

Lal, D. (1975): *Appraising Foreign Investment*, London: Heinemann
Educational Books.

Lal, D. (1980): *Prices for Planning*, London: Heinemann
Educational Books.

Lal, D. (1987): 'The Political Economy of Economic
Liberalization', *World Bank Economic Review*, Vol. 1, No. 2,
reprinted in Lal (1993).

Lal, D. (1989): *The Hindu Equilibrium*, 2 Vols., Oxford: Clarendon
Press.

Lal, D. (1993): *The Repressed Economy*, Economists of the 20th
century series, Aldershot: Edward Elgar.

Lal, D. (1994): *Against Dirigisme*, ICEG, San Francisco: ICS Press.

Lal, D. (1994a): 'In Praise of the Classics', in G. Meier (ed.), *From
Classical Economics to Development Economics*, New York: St.
Martin's Press, pp. 28–50.

Lal, D. (1994b): 'Poverty and Development', in H. Siebert (ed.),
The Ethical Foundations of the Market Economy, Tübingen:
J. C. B. Mohr, pp. 147–73.

Lal, D. (1995): 'Eco-Fundamentalism', *International Affairs*, Vol.
71, No. 3, pp. 515–28.

Lal, D. (1995a): 'India and China – Contrasts in Economic
Liberalisation?', *World Development*, Vol. 23, September,
pp. 1,475–94.

Lal, D. (1998): *Unintended Consequences: Factor Endowments,
Culture and Politics*, the 1995 Ohlin Memorial Lectures,
Cambridge, Mass.: MIT Press.

Lal, D. and S. Maxfield (1993): 'The Political Economy of
Stabilization in Brazil', in A. Krueger and R. Bates (eds.):
Political and Economic Interactions in Economic Policy, Oxford:
Blackwell, reprinted in Lal (1993).

Lal, D., and H. Myint (1996): *The Political Economy of Poverty,
Equity and Growth – A Comparative Study*, Oxford: Clarendon
Press.

Lal, D. and S. van Wijnbergen (1985): 'Government deficits, the

real interest rate and LDC debt: On Global Crowding Out',
European Economic Review, Vol. 29, reprinted in Lal (1993).

Lal, D. and M. Wolf (1986): *Stagflation, Savings and the State*,
Oxford: Oxford University Press.

Letwin, S. (1992) : *The Anatomy of Thatcherism*, London: Fontana.

Levine, R., and D. Renelt (1992): 'A sensitivity analysis of cross-
country growth regressions', *American Economic Review*, Vol.
82, September, pp. 942-64.

Little, I. M. D. (1982): *Economic Development*, New York: Basic
Books.

Little, I. M. D. (1994) 'Trade and Industrialisation Revisited',
Iqbal Memorial Lecture, Pakistan Institute of Development
Economics, April.

Little, I. M. D., R. Cooper, W. M. Corden, and S. Rajapatirana
(1993): *Booms, Crisis and Adjustment: the Macroeconomic
Experience of Developing Countries*, New York: Oxford
University Press.

Lucas Jnr., R. E. (1988): 'The Mechanics of Economic
Development', *Journal of Monetary Economics*, Vol. 22, July,
pp. 3–42.

Maddison, A. (1989): *The World Economy in the 20th Century*,
Paris: OECD.

McBean, A. (1966): *Export Instability and Economic Development*,
Cambridge, Mass.: Harvard University Press.

Murphy, K. M., A. Shleifer and R. W Vishny (1989):
'Industrialisation and the Big Push', *Journal of Political
Economy*, Vol. 97, No. 5, October, pp. 1,003-26.

Newbery, D. and N. Stern (1987): *The Theory of Taxation for
Developing Countries*, Oxford: Oxford University Press.

Newbery, D. M. G. and J. E. Stiglitz (1981): *The Theory of*

Commodity Price Stabilisation, Oxford: Clarendon Press.

Nordhaus, W. D. (1994): *Managing the Global Commons*, Cambridge, Mass.: MIT Press.

North, D. C. (1990): *Institutions, Institutional Change and Economic Performance*, Cambridge: Cambridge University Press.

Oakeshott, M. (1975): *On Human Conduct*, Oxford: Clarendon Press.

Oakeshott, M. (1993): *Morality and Politics in Modern Europe*, New Haven, Conn.: Yale University Press.

Pack, H. (1994): 'Endogenous Growth Theory: Intellectual Appeal and Empirical Shortcomings', *Journal of Economic Perspectives*, Vol. 8, No. 1, pp. 55–72.

Reynolds, L. G. (1985): *Economic Growth in the Third World*, New Haven, Conn.: Yale University Press.

Ridley, M. (1995): *Down to Earth*, IEA Studies on the Environment No. 3, London: The Institute of Economic Affairs.

Romer, Paul M. (1986): 'Increasing Returns and Long Run Growth', *Journal of Political Economy*, Vol. 94, No. 5, October pp. 1002–36.

Sala-i-Martin, X. (1994): 'Cross-sectional regressions and the empirics of economic growth', *European Economic Review*, Vol. 38, Nos. 3/4, April, pp. 739–47.

Scott, M. Fg. (1989): *A New View of Economic Growth*, Oxford: Clarendon Press.

Sell, F. (1988): 'True Exposure: The Analysis of Trade Liberalisation in a General Equilibrium Framework', *Welwirtschaftliches Archiv*, Vol. 124, No. 4.

Sen, A. K. (1983): 'The Profit Motive', *Lloyds Bank Review*, January.

Sen, A. K. (1992): *Inequality Reexamined*, Cambridge, Mass.: Harvard University Press.

Simon, J. L. (1991): *The Economic Consequences of Immigration*, Oxford: Blackwell.

Solow, R. (1994): 'Perspectives on Growth Theory', *Journal of Economic Perspectives*, Vol. 8, No. 1, pp. 45–54.

Srinivasan, T. N. (1994): 'Destitution: A Discourse', *Journal of Economic Literature*, Vol. 32, December pp. 1,842–55.

Stern, N. (1991): 'The Determinants of Growth', *Economic Journal*, Vol. 101, January, pp. 122–33.

Stiglitz, J. (1986): 'The New Development Economics', *World Development*, Vol. 14, No. 2, February, pp. 257–65.

Stiglitz, J. (1994): *Whither Socialism?*, Cambridge, Mass.: MIT Press.

Subramanian, S. and A. Deaton (1996): 'The Demand for Food and Calories', *Journal of Political Economy*, Vol. 10, No. 1, February, pp. 133-62.

Sugden, R. (1992): 'A Review of Inequality Reexamined by Amartya Sen', *Journal of Economic Literature*, Vol. 31, December, pp. 1,947–68.

Tullock, G. (1967): 'Welfare costs of tariffs, monopolies and theft', *Western Economic journal*, Vol. 5, June, pp. 224–32.

Wade, R. (1990): *Governing the Market*, Princeton, NJ: Princeton University Press.

Williamson, J. (1990): *Latin American Adjustment*, Washington DC: Institute of International Economics.

World Bank (1991): *World Development Report 1991*, New York: Oxford University Press.

World Bank (1993): *The East Asian Miracle*, New York: Oxford University Press.

World Bank (1994): *Adjustment in Africa*, New York: Oxford University Press.

World Bank (1995): *World Debt Tables 1995*, Vol. 1, Washington D.C.: World Bank.

Wrigley, E. A. (1988): *Continuity, Chance and Change: The Character of the Industrial Revolution in England*, Cambridge: Cambridge University Press.

Young, A. (1992): 'A Tale of Two Cities: Factor Accumulation and Technical Change in Hong Kong and Singapore', in O. J. Blanchard and S. Fischer (eds.): *NBER Macroeconomics Annual 1992*, Cambridge, Mass.: MIT Press.

ABOUT THE IEA

The Institute is a research and educational charity (No. CC 235 351), limited by guarantee. Its mission is to improve understanding of the fundamental institutions of a free society with particular reference to the role of markets in solving economic and social problems.

The IEA achieves its mission by:

- a high-quality publishing programme
- conferences, seminars, lectures and other events
- outreach to school and college students
- brokering media introductions and appearances

The IEA, which was established in 1955 by the late Sir Antony Fisher, is an educational charity, not a political organisation. It is independent of any political party or group and does not carry on activities intended to affect support for any political party or candidate in any election or referendum, or at any other time. It is financed by sales of publications, conference fees and voluntary donations.

In addition to its main series of publications the IEA also publishes a quarterly journal, *Economic Affairs*, and has two specialist programmes – Environment and Technology, and Education.

The IEA is aided in its work by a distinguished international Academic Advisory Council and an eminent panel of Honorary Fellows. Together with other academics, they review prospective IEA publications, their comments being passed on anonymously to authors. All IEA papers are therefore subject to the same rigorous independent refereeing process as used by leading academic journals.

IEA publications enjoy widespread classroom use and course adoptions in schools and universities. They are also sold throughout the world and often translated/reprinted.

Since 1974 the IEA has helped to create a world-wide network of 100 similar institutions in over 70 countries. They are all independent but share the IEA's mission.

Views expressed in the IEA's publications are those of the authors, not those of the Institute (which has no corporate view), its Managing Trustees, Academic Advisory Council members or senior staff.

Members of the Institute's Academic Advisory Council, Honorary Fellows, Trustees and Staff are listed on the following page.

The Institute gratefully acknowledges financial support for its publications programme and other work from a generous benefaction by the late Alec and Beryl Warren.

Other papers recently published by the IEA include:

WHO, What and Why?

Transnational Government, Legitimacy and the World Health Organization
Roger Scruton
Occasional Paper 113; ISBN 0 255 36487 3
£8.00

The World Turned Rightside Up

A New Trading Agenda for the Age of Globalisation
John C. Hulsman
Occasional Paper 114; ISBN 0 255 36495 4
£8.00

The Representation of Business in English Literature

Introduced and edited by Arthur Pollard
Readings 53; ISBN 0 255 36491 1
£12.00

Anti-Liberalism 2000

The Rise of New Millennium Collectivism
David Henderson
Occasional Paper 115; ISBN 0 255 36497 0
£7.50

Capitalism, Morality and Markets
Brian Griffiths, Robert A. Sirico, Norman Barry & Frank Field
Readings 54; ISBN 0 255 36496 2
£7.50

A Conversation with Harris and Seldon
Ralph Harris & Arthur Seldon
Occasional Paper 116; ISBN 0 255 36498 9
£7.50

Malaria and the DDT Story
Richard Tren & Roger Bate
Occasional Paper 117; ISBN 0 255 36499 7
£10.00

A Plea to Economists Who Favour Liberty:
Assist the Everyman
Daniel B. Klein
Occasional Paper 118; ISBN 0 255 36501 2
£10.00

Waging the War of Ideas
John Blundell
Occasional Paper 119; ISBN 0 255 36500 4
£10.00

The Changing Fortunes of Economic Liberalism

Yesterday, Today and Tomorrow
David Henderson
Occasional Paper 105 (new edition); ISBN 0 255 36520 9
£12.50

The Global Education Industry

Lessons from Private Education in Developing Countries
James Tooley
Hobart Paper 141 (new edition); ISBN 0 255 36503 9
£12.50

Saving Our Streams

The Role of the Anglers' Conservation Association in
Protecting English and Welsh Rivers
Roger Bate
Research Monograph 53; ISBN 0 255 36494 6
£10.00

Better Off Out?

The Benefits or Costs of EU Membership
Brian Hindley & Martin Howe
Occasional Paper 99 (new edition); ISBN 0 255 36502 0
£10.00

Buckingham at 25

Freeing the Universities from State Control

Edited by James Tooley

Readings 55; ISBN 0 255 36512 8

£15.00

Lectures on Regulatory and Competition Policy

Irwin M. Stelzer

Occasional Paper 120; ISBN 0 255 36511 X

£12.50

Misguided Virtue

False Notions of Corporate Social Responsibility

David Henderson

Hobart Paper 142; ISBN 0 255 36510 1

£12.50

HIV and Aids in Schools

The Political Economy of Pressure Groups and Miseducation

Barrie Craven, Pauline Dixon, Gordon Stewart & James Tooley

Occasional Paper 121; ISBN 0 255 36522 5

£10.00

The Road to Serfdom

The Reader's Digest *condensed version*
Friedrich A. Hayek
Occasional Paper 122; ISBN 0 255 36530 6
£7.50

Bastiat's *The Law*

Introduction by Norman Barry
Occasional Paper 123; ISBN 0 255 36509 8
£7.50

A Globalist Manifesto for Public Policy

Charles Calomiris
Occasional Paper 124; ISBN 0 255 36525 X
£7.50

Euthanasia for Death Duties

Putting Inheritance Tax Out of Its Misery
Barry Bracewell-Milnes
Research Monograph 54; ISBN 0 255 36513 6
£10.00

Liberating the Land

The Case for Private Land-use Planning
Mark Pennington
Hobart Paper 143; ISBN 0 255 36508 X
£10.00

IEA Yearbook of Government Performance 2002/2003

Edited by Peter Warburton
Yearbook 1; ISBN 0 255 36532 2
£15.00

Britain's Relative Economic Performance, 1870–1999

Nicholas Crafts
Research Monograph 55; ISBN 0 255 36524 1
£10.00

Should We Have Faith in Central Banks?

Otmar Issing
Occasional Paper 125; ISBN 0 255 36528 4
£7.50

The Dilemma of Democracy
Arthur Seldon
Hobart Paper 136 (reissue); ISBN 0 255 36536 5
£10.00

Capital Controls: A 'Cure' Worse Than the Problem?
Forrest Capie
Research Monograph 56; ISBN 0 255 36506 3
£10.00

To order copies of currently available IEA papers, or to enquire about availability, please write (no postage required from within the UK) to:

Lavis Marketing
IEA orders
FREEPOST LON21280
Oxford OX3 7BR

Or contact Lavis Marketing on:
Tel: 01865 767575
Fax: 01865 750079
Email: orders@lavismarketing.co.uk

The IEA also offers a subscription service to its publications. For a single annual payment, currently £40.00 in the UK, you will receive every title the IEA publishes across the course of a year, invitations to events, and discounts on our extensive back catalogue. For more information, please contact:

Subscriptions
The Institute of Economic Affairs
2 Lord North Street
London SW1P 3LB

Tel: 020 7799 8900
Fax: 020 7799 2137
Website: www.iea.org.uk